The Quare Fellow and The Hostage

The Quare Fellow

and

The Hostage

Two plays by

Brendan Behan

An Evergreen Black Cat Book

GROVE PRESS, INC. NEW YORK

ACKNOWLEDGMENT: Cover photograph through courtesy of Spoken Arts, Inc., whose recording of *Brendan Behan Sings Irish Folksongs and Ballads* introduces a literary talent whose performance is passionate, dazzling and uproariously funny.

First Evergreen Black Cat Edition 1964
Third Printing

MANUFACTURED IN THE UNITED STATES OF AMERICA

Contents

The Quare Fellow

This version of "The Quare Fellow" was first presented by Theatre Workshop at the Theatre Royal, Stratford, London, E.15, on 24th May 1956, with the following cast:

PRISONERS

Dunlavin	Maxwell Shaw
Neighbour	Gerard Dynevor
Prisoner A. (Hard Case)	Glynn Edwards
Prisoner B. (The Man of Thirty)	Brian Murphy
Lifer	Bill Grover
The Other Fellow	Ron Brooker
Mickser	Eric Ogle
English Voice	John Rutley
Scholara (*Young Prisoners*)	Timothy Harley
Shaybo (*Young Prisoners*)	George Eugeniou
Prisoner C. (The Boy from the Island)	Henry Livings
Prisoner D. (The Embezzler)	Barry Clayton
Prisoner E. (The Bookie)	Brian Murphy

WARDERS

Chief Warder	Maxwell Shaw
Regan	Dudley Foster
Crimmin	Brian Nunn
Donelly (Warder 1)	Clive Goodwin
The New One (Warder 2)	Fred Cooper
The Prison Governor	Robert Henderson
Holy Healey	Barry Clayton
The Hangman	Gerry Raffles
Jenkinson	Brian Murphy

The play directed by Joan Littlewood

ACT I

A prisoner sings: he is in one of the punishment cells.

A hungry feeling came o'er me stealing
And the mice were squealing in my prison cell,
And that old triangle
Went jingle jangle,
Along the banks of the Royal Canal.

The curtain rises.

The scene is the bottom floor or landing of a wing in a city prison, "B.1". The cell doors are of metal with a card giving the name, age and religion of the occupant. Two of the cells have no cards. The left of the stage leads to the circle, the administrative heart of the prison, and on the right, in the wall and at right angles to the audience, is a window, from which a view may be had of the laundry yard of the women's prison. On the wall and facing the audience is printed in large block shaded Victorian lettering the word "SILENCE".

PRISONER.

To begin the morning
The warder bawling
Get out of bed and clean up your cell,
And that old triangle
Went jingle jangle,
Along the banks of the Royal Canal.

A triangle is beaten, loudly and raucously. A WARDER *comes briskly and, swinging a bunch of keys, goes to the vacant cells, looks in the spyholes, takes two white cards from his pocket, and puts one on each door. Then he goes to the other doors, looks in the spyholes and unlocks them.*

Meanwhile the singer in the base punishment cells is on his third verse:

The screw was peeping
And the lag was weeping . . .

But this only gets as far as the second line, for the warder leans over the stairs and shouts down . . .

WARDER. The screw is listening as well as peeping, and you'll be bloody well weeping if you don't give over your moaning. We might go down there and give you something to moan about. [*The singing stops and he turns and shouts up and down the landing.*] B. Wings: two, three and one. Stand to your doors. Come on, clean up your cells there. [*He goes off* R.]

PRISONERS A. *and* B. *come out of their cells, collect buckets and brushes, and start the morning's chores.* A. *is a man of 40, he has done two "laggings", a sentence of five years or more, and some preventive detention.* B. *is a gentle-looking man and easy-going.*

PRISONER A. Nice day for the races.

PRISONER B. Don't think I can make it today. Too much to do in the office. Did you hear the commotion last night round in D. Wing? A reprieve must have come through.

PRISONER A. Aye, but there's two for a haircut and shave, I wonder which one's been chucked?

PRISONER B. Dunlavin might know; give him a call there.

PRISONER A. Dunlavin!

VOICE [*from cell*].

> There are hands that will welcome you in
> There are lips that I am burning to kiss
> There are two eyes that shine . . .

PRISONER A. Hey, Dunlavin, are you going to scrub that place of yours away?

VOICE.

> Far away where the blue shadows fall
> I will come to contentment and rest,
> And the toils of the day
> Will be all charmed away . . .

PRISONER A. Hey, Dunlavin.

DUNLAVIN *appears in the door of the cell polishing a large enamel chamber pot with a cloth. An old man, he has spent most of his life in jail. Unlike most old lags he has not become absolutely dulled from imprisonment.*

DUNLAVIN. . . . In my little grey home in the West.

PRISONER A. What do you think that is you're polishing—the Railway Cup?

DUNLAVIN. I'm shining this up for a special visitor. Healey of the Department of Justice is coming up today to inspect the cells.

PRISONER A. Will he be round again so soon?

DUNLAVIN. He's always round the day before an execution. I think he must be in the hanging and flogging section.

PRISONER B. Dunlavin, there you are, at the corner of the wing, with the joints in the hot-water pipes bringing you news from every art and part, any time you put your ear to it.

DUNLAVIN. Well? Well?

PRISONER B. Well, what was the commotion last night round in D. Wing? Did the quare fellow get a reprieve?

DUNLAVIN. Just a minute till I put back me little bit of china, and I'll return and tell all. Now which quare fellow do you mean? The fellow beat his wife to death with the silver-topped cane, that was a presentation to him from the Combined Staffs, Excess and Refunds branch of the late Great Southern Railways, was reprieved, though why him any more than the other fellow is more nor I can tell.

PRISONER A. Well, I suppose they looked at it, he only killed her and left it at that. He didn't cut the corpse up afterwards with a butcher's knife.

DUNLAVIN. Yes, and then of course the other fellow used a meat-chopper. Real bog-man act. Nearly as bad as a shotgun, or getting the weed-killer mixed up in the stir-about. But a man with a silver-topped cane, that's a man that's a cut above meat-choppers whichever way you look at it.

PRISONER A. Well, I suppose we can expect Silver-top round soon to start his life.

PRISONER B. Aye, we've a couple of vacancies.

PRISONER A. There's a new card up here already.

DUNLAVIN. I declare to God you're right. [*Goes to read one of the cards.*] It's not him at all, it's another fellow, doing two year, for . . . oh, the dirty beast, look what the dirty man-beast is in for. 'Clare to God, putting the likes of that beside me. They must think this is the bloody sloblands.

PRISONER B. There's another fellow here.

DUNLAVIN. I hope it's not another of that persuasion. [*Reads the card.*] Ah, no, it's only the murderer, thanks be to God.

The others have a read of the card and skip back to their own cells.

DUNLAVIN. You wouldn't mind old Silver-top. Killing your wife is a natural class of a thing could happen to the best of us. But this other dirty animal on me left . . .

PRISONER B. Ah well, now he's here he'll just have to do his birdlime like anyone else.

DUNLAVIN. That doesn't say that he should do it in the next flowery dell to me. Robbers, thieves and murderers I can abide, but when it comes to that class of carry-on— Good night, Joe Doyle.

PRISONER A. [*indicates 22*]. This fellow was dead lucky.

PRISONER B. Live lucky.

PRISONER A. Two fellows waiting to be topped and he's the one that gets away. As a general rule they don't like reprieving one and topping the other.

DUNLAVIN. So as to be on the safe side, and not to be making fish of one and flesh of the other, they usually top both. Then, of course, the Minister might have said, enough is as good as a feast.

They rest on their brooms.

PRISONER B. It must be a great thing to be told at the last minute that you're not going to be topped after all. To be lying there sweating and watching. The two screws for the death watch coming on at twelve o'clock and the two going off shaking hands with you, and you go to bed, and stare up at the ceiling.

DUNLAVIN. And the two screws nod to each other across the fire to make a sup of tea, but to do it easy in case they wake you, and you turn round in the bed towards the fire and you say "I'll take a sup as you're at it" and one of the screws says "Ah, so you're awake, Mick. We were just wetting it; isn't it a good job you spoke up in time."

PRISONER A. And after that, the tea is drunk and they offer you cigarettes, though the mouth is burned off you from smoking and anyway you've more than they have, you've got that many you'll be leaving them after you, and you lie down and get up, and get up and lie down, and the two screws not letting on to be minding you and not taking their eyes off you for one half-minute, and you walk up and down a little bit more . . .

PRISONER B. And they ask you would you like another game of draughts or would you sooner write a letter, and getting on to morning you hear a bell out in the city, and you ask them the time, but they won't tell you.

DUNLAVIN. But they put a good face on it, and one says "There's that old watch stopped again" and he says to the other screw "Have you your watch, Jack?" and the other fellow makes a great joke of it, "I'll have to take a run up as far as the North City Pawn shop and ask them to let me have a look at it." And then the door is unlocked and everyone sweats blood, and they come in and ask your man to stand up a minute, that's if he's able, while they read him something: "I am instructed to inform you that the Minister has, he hasn't, he has, he hasn't recommended to the President, that . . ."

PRISONER A. And the quare fellow says "Did you say 'has recommended or has not recommended. . . ?' I didn't quite catch that."

DUNLAVIN. My bloody oath but he catches it. Although I remember once in a case like now when there were two fellows to be topped over two different jobs, didn't the bloody fellow from the Prison Board, as it was then, in old Max Greeb's time, didn't he tell the wrong man he was reprieved? Your man was delighted for a few hours and then they had to go back and tell him "Sorry, my mistake, but you're to be topped after all"?

PRISONER B. And the fellow that was reprieved, I bet he was glad.

DUNLAVIN. Of course he was glad, anyone that says that a condemned man would be better off hung than doing life, let them leave it to his own discretion. Do you know who feels it worse going out to be topped?

PRISONER A. Corkmen and Northerners . . . they've such bloody hard necks.

DUNLAVIN. I have to do me funny half-hour for Holy Healey. I'm talking serious now.

PRISONER A. All right, come on, let's have it—

DUNLAVIN. The man that feels it worst, going into that little house with the red door and the silver painted gates at the bottom of D. Wing, is a man that has been in the nick before, when some other merchant was topped; or he's heard screws or old lags in the bag shop or at exercise talking about it. A new chap that's never done anything but murder, and that only once, is usually a respectable man, such as this Silver-top here. He knows nothing about it, except the few lines that he'd see in the papers. "Condemned man entered the hang-house at seven fifty-nine. At eight three the doctor pronounced life extinct."

PRISONER B. That's a lot of mullarkey. In the first place the doctor has his back turned after the trap goes down, and doesn't turn and face it until a screw has caught the rope and stopped it wriggling. Then they go out and lock up the shop and have their breakfast and don't come back for an hour. Then they cut your man down and the doctor slits the back of his neck to see if the bones are broken. Who's to know what happens in the hour your man is swinging there, maybe wriggling to himself in the pit.

PRISONER A. You're right there. When I was in the nick in England, there was a screw doing time, he'd been smuggling out medical reports on hangings and selling them to the Sunday papers, and he told me that one bloke had lived seventeen minutes at the end of a rope.

DUNLAVIN. I don't believe that! Seventeen minutes is a bloody long time to be hanging on the end of a rope.

PRISONER A. It was their own medical report.

PRISONER B. I'll lay odds to a make that Silver-top isn't half charmed with himself he's not going with the meat-chopper in the morning.

DUNLAVIN. You could sing that if you had an air to it.

PRISONER A. They'll have him down to reception, changed into Fry's and over here any time now.

DUNLAVIN. Him and this other jewel here. Bad an' all as Silver-top was to beat his wife's brains out, I'd as lief have him near to me as this article. Dirty beast! I won't have an hour's luck for the rest of me six months, and me hoping to touch Uncle Healey today for a letter to the Room-Keepers for when I'd go out.

PRISONER B. Eh, Dunlavin, is the Department trying to reform, reconstruct and rehabilitate you in your old age?

DUNLAVIN. Ah no, it's nothing to do with the Department. Outside his job in the Department, Uncle Healey's in some holy crowd, that does good be stealth. They never let the right hand know what the left hand doeth, as the man said. Of course they never put either hand in their pocket, so you'd never get money off them, but they can give letters to the Prisoners' Aid and the Room-Keepers. Mind you. Healey's not here today as a holy man. He'll just be fixing up the man that's getting hung in the morning, but if I can get on the right side of him, he might mix business with pleasure and give me a letter for when I get out.

PRISONER B. Now we know the cause of all the spring-cleaning.

DUNLAVIN. And a fellow in the kitchen told us they're doing a special dinner for us on account of Uncle Healey's visit.

PRISONER A. Do you mean we're getting food with our meals today?

DUNLAVIN. That's right, and I can't be standing yapping to youse. I've to hang up my holy pictures and think up a few funny remarks for him. God, what Jimmie O'Dea is getting thousands for I've to do for a pair of old socks and a ticket for the Prisoners' Aid.

DUNLAVIN *goes into his cell. Two* YOUNG PRISONERS *aged about seventeen go past with sweeping brushes in front of them, singing softly and in unison.*

YOUNG PRISONERS.

Only one more cell inspection
We go out next Saturday,
Only one more cell inspection
And we go far, far away.

PRISONER A. What brings you fellows round here this morning?

YOUNG PRISONER 1. Our screw told us to sweep all round the Juvenile Wing and then to come round here and give it a bit of a going over.

PRISONER B. And have you your own wing done?

YOUNG PRISONER 2. No, but if we did our wing first, we'd miss the mots hanging out the laundry. You can't see them from our wing.

PRISONER A. Just as well, maybe; you're bad enough as it is.

YOUNG PRISONER 1. But I tell you what you will see from our wing this morning. It's the carpenter bringing up the coffin for the quare fellow and leaving it over in the mortuary to have it handy for the morning. There's two orderlies besides us over in the Juveniles, and we were going to toss up who'd come over here, but they're country fellows and they'd said they'd sooner see the coffin. I'd sooner a pike at a good-looking mot than the best coffin in Ireland, wouldn't you, Shaybo?

YOUNG PRISONER 2. Certainly I would, and outside that, when you're over here, there's always a chance of getting a bit of education about screwing jobs, and suchlike, from experienced men. Do you think Triplex or celluloid is the best for Yale locks, sir?

YOUNG PRISONER 1. Do you carry the stick all the time, sir?

PRISONER A. If I had a stick I'd know where to put it, across your bloody . . .

YOUNG PRISONER 2. Scholara, get sweeping, here's the screw.

They drift off sweeping and singing softly.

PRISONER B. He's bringing one of 'em. Is it Silver-top or the other fellow?

PRISONER A. Silver-top. I remember him being half carried into the circle the night he was sentenced to death.

PRISONER B. He has a right spring in his step this morning then.

PRISONER A. He's not looking all that happy. Still, I suppose he hasn't got over the shock yet.

WARDER *and a* PRISONER *come on* L. *The* PRISONER *is in early middle age; when he speaks he has a "good accent". He is carrying a pillow slip which contains his sheets and other kit. The* WARDER *halts him.*

WARDER REGAN. Stand by the door with your name on it. Later on when you've seen the doctor these fellows will show you how to lay your kit. Stand there now, till the doctor is ready to see you. [*He goes. There is a pause, while the* PRISONERS *survey the newcomer.*]

PRISONER B. He'll bloody well cheer the place up, won't he?

LIFER. Have any of you got a cigarette?

PRISONER A. That's a good one. You're not in the condemned cell now, you know. No snout allowed here.

PRISONER B. Unless you manage to scrounge a dog-end off the remands.

PRISONER A. Or pick one up in the exercise yard after a man the like of yourself that's allowed them as a special concession. Not, by God, that we picked up much after you. What did you do with your dog-ends?

LIFER. Threw them in the fire.

PRISONER B. You what!

PRISONER A. How was it the other poor bastard, that's got no reprieve and is to be topped in the morning—how was it he was always able to leave a trail of butts behind him when he went off exercise?

LIFER. I've never been in prison before; how was I to know?

PRISONER A. You're a curse of God liar, my friend, you did know; for it was whispered to him by the fellows from the hospital bringing over the grub to the condemned cell. He never gave them as much as a match! And he couldn't even bring his dog-ends to the exercise yard and drop them behind for us to pick up when we came out later.

PRISONER B. I bet you're charmed with yourself that you're not going through the iron door tomorrow morning.

The LIFER *doesn't speak, but looks down at his suit.*

PRISONER A. Aye, you're better off in that old suit, bad as it is, than the wooden overcoat the quare fellow is going to get tomorrow morning.

PRISONER B. The longest you could do would be twenty years. More than likely you'll get out in half of that. Last man to finish up in the Bog, he done eleven.

LIFER. Eleven. How do you live through it?

PRISONER A. A minute at a time.

PRISONER B. You haven't got a bit of snout for him, have you? [PRISONER A. *shakes his head.*] Maybe Dunlavin has. Hey, Dunlavin, have you e'er a smoke you'd give this chap? Hey, Dunlavin.

DUNLAVIN [*coming from his cell*]. Yes, what is it? Anyone there the name of headache?

PRISONER B. Could you manage to give this chap something to smoke? E'er a bit of snout at all.

DUNLAVIN. There's only one brand of tobacco allowed here—"Three Nuns". None today, none tomorrow, and none the day after.

He goes back into his cell.

PRISONER B. Eh, Dunlavin, come back to hell out of that.

DUNLAVIN. Well, what?

PRISONER B. This poor chap after being smoking about sixty a day . . .

DUNLAVIN. Where?

PRISONER B. In the condemned cell—where else?

DUNLAVIN. Now I have you. Sure I thought you were the other fellow, and you're not, you're only the murderer. God comfort you. [*Shakes hands.*] Certainly so. [*Takes off his jacket, looks up and down the wing, undoes his trousers and from the depths of his combinations he produces a cigarette end, and a match, and presents them to the* LIFER.] Reprieved in the small hours of this morning. Certainly so. The dead arose and appeared to many, as the man said, but you'll be getting yourself a bad name standing near that other fellow's door. This is your flowery dell, see? It has your name there on that little card. And all your particulars. Age forty-three. Religion R.C.

LIFER [*reads*]. Life.

DUNLAVIN. And a bloody sight better than death any day of the week.

PRISONER B. It always says that. The Governor will explain it all to you later this morning.

DUNLAVIN. Or maybe they'll get holy Uncle Healey to do it.

PRISONER B. Go into your cell and have a smoke for yourself. Bring in your kit bag. [*Passes in kit to* LIFER.] Have a quiet burn there before the screw comes round; we'll keep nick. [LIFER *closes the door of his cell.*]

DUNLAVIN. God knows I got the pick of good neighbours. Lovely people. Give me a decent murderer though, rather then the likes of this other fellow. Well, I'll go into me little place and get on with me bit of dobying so as to have it all nice for Healey when he comes round. [He *goes back to his cell.*]

PRISONER B. [*to* LIFER]. Don't light up yet! Here's the screw coming.

PRISONER A. With the other fellow.

WARDER REGAN *and another prisoner, "the* OTHER FELLOW", *an anxious-faced man, wearing prison clothes and carrying a kit bag, come on* L.

WARDER REGAN. Yes, this is your flowery dell. Leave in your kitbag and stand at your door and wait for the doctor. These other fellows will show you where to go when he comes.

OTHER FELLOW. Right, sir. Very good, sir.

WARDER REGAN *goes, the* OTHER FELLOW *has a look round.*

PRISONER B. There's a bloke in the end cell getting himself a quiet burn. Why don't you join him before the screws get back?

The OTHER FELLOW *notices the card on* LIFER'S *cell.*

OTHER FELLOW. My God! Is this what I've come to, mixing with murderers! I'd rather not, thank you, though I could do with a smoke. I'll have to spend long months here, even if I get my remission, with murderers and thieves and God knows what! You're not all murderers are you? You haven't killed anyone, have you?

PRISONER B. Not for a while, I haven't.

OTHER FELLOW. I cannot imagine any worse crime than taking a life, can you?

PRISONER B. It'd depend whose life.

OTHER FELLOW. Of course. I mean, a murderer would be justified in taking his own life, wouldn't he? "We send him forth" says Carlisle—you've heard of Carlisle haven't you?—"We send him forth, back to the void, back to the darkness, far out beyond the stars. Let him go from us."

DUNLAVIN [*head out of door of cell*]. Oh. [*Looks at* OTHER FELLOW.] I thought it was Healey from the Department or someone giving it out of them.

PRISONER A. Looks like this man is a bit of an intellectual.

DUNLAVIN. Is that what they call it now?

LIFER. Thanks for the smoke, Mr. Dunlavin.

DUNLAVIN. Not at all, sure, you're welcome, call again when you're passing. But remember the next wife you kill and you getting forty fags a day in the condemned cell, think of them as is not so fortunate as yourself and leave a few dog-ends around the exercise yard after you. Here's these noisy little gets again.

The two YOUNG PRISONERS *come round from the left, their sweeping brushes in front of them and singing their song. The* OTHER FELLOW *stands quite still at his door.*

YOUNG PRISONERS.

Only one more cell inspection
We go out next Saturday
Only one more cell inspection
Then we go far far away.
[*They are sweeping near the* LIFER.]
Only one more cell inspection
We go out next Saturday
Only one more cell . . .

LIFER. For God's sake shut up that squeaking . . .

YOUNG PRISONER 1. We've as much right to open our mouth as what you have, and you only a wet day in the place.

PRISONER B. Leave the kids alone. You don't own the place, you know. They're doing no harm. [*To the* YOUNG PRISONERS.] You want to sweep this bit of floor away?

DUNLAVIN. What brings you round here so often? If you went over to the remand wings you might pick up a bit of snout or a look at the paper.

YOUNG PRISONER 1. We get a smoke and the *Mail* every day off a limey on our road that's on remand. He's in over the car smuggling. But round here this morning you can see the mots from the laundry over on the female side hanging out the washing in the exercise yard. Do youse look at them? I suppose when you get old, though, you don't much bother about women.

PRISONER B. I'm thirty-six, mac.

YOUNG PRISONER 1. Ah, I thought that. Don't suppose you care if you never see a mot. There's Shaybo there and he never thinks of anything else. Do you think of anything else but women, Shaybo?

YOUNG PRISONER 2. Yes. Robbing and stealing, Scholara. You go to the window and keep an eye out for them and I'll sweep on round here till you give us a call.

YOUNG PRISONER 1. Right, Shaybo, they should be nearly out now. [*Goes up and stands by window.*]

PRISONER B. I forgot about the women.

DUNLAVIN. I didn't. It's a great bit of a treat today—that and having me leg rubbed. Neighbour and I wait in for it.

YOUNG PRISONER 1 [*from the window, in a coarse whisper*]. Shaybo, you can see them now.

YOUNG PRISONER 2. The blondy one from North Crumlin?

YOUNG PRISONER 1. Yes, and there's another one with her. I don't know her.

YOUNG PRISONER 2. Must be a country mot. Scholara doesn't know her. Women.

DUNLAVIN. Women.

PRISONER A. I see the blondy one waving.

YOUNG PRISONER 1. If it's all the one to you, I'd like you to know that's my mot and it's me she's waving at.

PRISONER A. I'll wave you a thick ear.

DUNLAVIN. Hey, Neighbour! Where the hell is he this morning? Neighbour!

AN OLD MAN'S CREAKING VOICE. Here I am, Neighbour, here I am.

> NEIGHBOUR, *a bent old man, comes on from* L., *hobbling as quickly as he can on a stick.*

DUNLAVIN. Ah, you lost mass.

NEIGHBOUR. What, are they gone in already?

DUNLAVIN. No, but they're finished hanging up the top row of clothes. There'll be no stretching or reaching off chairs.

NEIGHBOUR. Still, thanks be to God for small mercies. They'll be out again this day week.

PRISONER A. If you lives to see it.

NEIGHBOUR. Why wouldn't I live to see it as well as what you would? This is not the nearest I was to fine women, nor are they the first good-looking ones I saw.

PRISONER A. With that old cough of yours they could easy be the last.

NEIGHBOUR. God, you're a desperate old gas bag. We remember better-looking women than ever they were, don't we, Dunlavin? Meena La Bloom, do you remember her?

DUNLAVIN. Indeed and I do; many's the seaman myself and Meena gave the hey and a do, and Mickey Finn to.

NEIGHBOUR. And poor May Oblong.

DUNLAVIN. Ah, where do you leave poor May? The Lord have mercy on her, wasn't I with her one night in the digs, and there was a Member of Parliament there, and May after locking him in the back room and taking away his trousers, with him going over the north wall that morning to vote for Home Rule. "For the love of your country and mine," he shouts under the door to May, "give me back me trousers." "So I will," says May, "if you shove a fiver out under the door."

NEIGHBOUR. He had the wad hid? Dirty suspicious old beast.

DUNLAVIN. That's right. He was cute enough to hide his wad somewhere, drunk and all as he was the previous night. All we got in his trousers was a locket of hair of the patriotic plumber of Dolphin's barn that swore to let his hair grow till Ireland was free.

NEIGHBOUR. Ah, poor May, God help her, she was the heart of the roll.

DUNLAVIN. And when she was arrested for carrying on after the curfew, the time of the trouble, she was fined for having concealed about her person two Thompson submachine guns, 1921 pattern, three Mills bombs, and a stick of dynamite.

NEIGHBOUR. And will you ever forget poor Lottie L'Estrange, that got had up for pushing the soldier into Spencer Dock?

DUNLAVIN. Ah, God be with the youth of us.

NEIGHBOUR. And Cork Annie, and Lady Limerick.

DUNLAVIN. And Julia Rice and the Goofy One.

NEIGHBOUR [*turns towards window*]. Hey, you, move out of the way there and give us a look. Dunlavin, come up here before they go, and have a look at the blondy one.

YOUNG PRISONER 1. Go 'long, you dirty old dog. That's my mot you're speaking about. [*Shoves* NEIGHBOUR.] You old heap of dirt, to wave at a decent girl.

PRISONER A. Hey, snots, d'you think you own the bloody place?

YOUNG PRISONER 1 Would you like it, to have that dirty old eyebox looking at your mot?

PRISONER B. He's not going to eat her.

DUNLAVIN [*from behind*]. No, but he'd like to.

YOUNG PRISONER 2. That's right, and Scholara is nearly married to her. At least she had a squealer for him and he has to pay her money every week. Any week he's outside like, to give it, or her to get it.

YOUNG PRISONER 1 [*blows a kiss*]. That's right, and I have him putting his rotten old eye on her.

OTHER FELLOW [*at his doorway*]. God preserve us.

PRISONER A. Well, you don't own the bloody window. [*Shoves* YOUNG PRISONER 1 *out of way and brings over* NEIGHBOUR.] Come on, you, if you want to see the May procession.

NEIGHBOUR. Ah, thanks, butty, your blood's worth bottling.

PRISONER A. I didn't do it on account of you, but if you let them young pups get away with too much they'd be running the place.

YOUNG PRISONER 2. Come on, Scholara, we'll mosey back. The screw will think we're lost.

They go back down the stairs, pick up their brushes, and start sweeping again and singing . . .

YOUNG PRISONER 1.

Only one more cell inspection
We go out next Saturday

YOUNG PRISONER 2.

Only one more cell inspection . . .

LIFER. Shut your bloody row, can't you?

DUNLAVIN. Shut up yourself; you're making more noise than any of them.

YOUNG PRISONER 1. Don't tell us to shut up, you bastard.

PRISONER B. Ah leave him alone; he started life this morning.

YOUNG PRISONER 1. Ah we're sorry, mister, ain't we, Shaybo?

YOUNG PRISONER 2. God, we are. Go over and take a pike at the female yard. They hang up the clothes now and Scholara's mot is over there. You can have a look at her. Scholara won't mind, will you, Schol?

YOUNG PRISONER 1. Certainly and I won't. Not with you going to the Bog to start life in a couple of days, where you won't see a woman.

YOUNG PRISONER 2. A child.

YOUNG PRISONER 1. A dog.

YOUNG PRISONER 2. A fire.

PRISONER A. Get to hell out of that round to your own wing. Wouldn't you think a man would know all that forbye you telling it to him?

YOUNG PRISONER 2. We were going anyway. We've seen all we wanted to see. It wasn't to look at a lot of old men we came here, but to see mots hanging out the washing.

YOUNG PRISONER 1. And eitherways, we'll be a lot nearer the women than you'll be next Saturday night. Think of us when you're sitting locked up in the old flowery, studying the Bible, Chapter 1, verse 2, and we trucking round in chase of charver.

They samba out with their brushes for partners, humming the Wedding Samba.

PRISONER A. Them young gets have too much old gab out of them altogether. I was a Y.P. in Walton before the war and I can tell you they'd be quiet boys if they got the larrying we used to get.

OTHER FELLOW. And talking so disrespectfully about the Bible.

NEIGHBOUR. Belied and they needn't; many's the time the Bible was a consolation to a fellow all alone in the old cell. The lovely thin paper with a bit of mattress coir in it, if you could get a match or a bit of tinder or any class of light, was as good a smoke as ever I tasted. Am I right, Dunlavin?

DUNLAVIN. Damn the lie, Neighbour. The first twelve months I done, I smoked my way half-way through the book of Genesis and three inches of my mattress. When the Free State came in we were afraid of our life they were going to change the mattresses for feather beds. And you couldn't smoke feathers, not, be God, if they were rolled in the Song of Solomon itself. But sure, thanks to God, the Free State didn't change anything more than the badge on the warders' caps.

OTHER FELLOW. Can I be into my cell for a while?

PRISONER B. Until the doctor calls you. [*Goes into his cell.*]

PRISONER A. Well, I'm going to have a rest. It's hard work doing a lagging.

LIFER. A lagging? That's penal servitude, isn't it?

DUNLAVIN. Three years or anything over.

LIFER. Three years is a long time.

DUNLAVIN. I wouldn't like to be that long hanging.

NEIGHBOUR. Is he the . . .

DUNLAVIN [*sotto voce*]. Silver-top! [*Aloud.*] Started life this morning.

NEIGHBOUR. So they're not going to top you after all? Well, you're a lucky man. I worked one time in the hospital, helping the screw there, and the morning of the execution he gave me two bottles of stout to take the hood off the fellow was after being topped. I wouldn't have done it a second time for two glasses of malt, no, nor a bottle of it. I cut the hood away; his head was all twisted and his face black, but the two eyes were the worst; like a rabbit's; it was fear that had done it.

LIFER. Perhaps he didn't feel anything. How do you know?

NEIGHBOUR. I only seen him. I never had a chance of asking him. [NEIGHBOUR *goes to the murderer's door.*] Date of expiration of sentence, life. In some ways I wouldn't mind if that was my lot. What do you say?

DUNLAVIN. I don't know; it's true we're too old and bet for lobbywatching and shaking down anywhere, so that you'd fall down and sleep on the pavement of a winter's night and not know but you were lying snug and comfortable in the Shelbourne.

NEIGHBOUR. Only then to wake up on some lobby and the hard floorboards under you, and a lump of hard filth for your pillow, and the cold and the drink shaking you, wishing it was morning for the market pubs to open, where if you had the price of a drink you could sit in the warm anyway. Except, God look down on you, if it was Sunday.

DUNLAVIN. Ah, there's the agony. No pub open, but the bells battering your bared nerves and all you could do with the cold and the sickness was to lean over on your side and wish that God would call you.

LIFER. If I was outside my life wouldn't be like that.

NEIGHBOUR. No, but ours would.

DUNLAVIN [*quietly*]. See, we're selfish, mister, like everyone else.

WARDER [*shouts off*]. Medical applications and receptions. Fall in for the doctor. [LIFER *looks lost.*]

DUNLAVIN. Yes, that's you. Go up there to the top of the wing and wait there till the screw tells you to go in. Neighbour, call them other fellows.

Exit LIFER.

NEIGHBOUR. Come on—the vet's here.

DUNLAVIN [*calling in to the* OTHER FELLOW]. Hey, come out and get gelded.

OTHER FELLOW *and* PRISONERS A. *and* B. *come out of cells.*

NEIGHBOUR. You're for the doctor. Go on up there with the rest of them. Me and Dunlavin don't go up. We only wait to be rubbed.

DUNLAVIN. Don't have any chat at all with that fellow. D'you see what he's in for?

NEIGHBOUR *goes and looks. Exit* OTHER FELLOW *and* PRISONERS A. *and* B.

NEIGHBOUR. What the hell does that mean?

DUNLAVIN. A bloody sex mechanic.

NEIGHBOUR. I didn't know.

DUNLAVIN. Well, you know now. I'll go in and get me chair. You can sit on it after me. It'll save you bringing yours out.

NEIGHBOUR. Well, if you go first and you have a chance of a go at the spirit bottle, don't swig the bloody lot. Remember I'm for treatment too.

DUNLAVIN. Don't be such an old begrudger. He'll bring a quart bottle of it, and who could swallow that much methylated spirit in the few drops you'd get at it?

NEIGHBOUR. You could, or a bucket of it, if it was lying anywhere handy. I seen you do it, bluestone and all, only buns to a bear as far as you were concerned.

DUNLAVIN. Do you remember the old doctor they had here years ago?

NEIGHBOUR. The one they used to call Crippen.

DUNLAVIN. The very man. There was one day I was brought in for drinking the chat and I went to court that morning and was here in the afternoon still as drunk as Pontius Pilate. Crippen was examining me. "When I put me hand there you cough," and all to that effect. "Did you ever have V.D.?" says he. "I haven't got your habits," says I to him. These fellows weren't long.

Re-enter PRISONERS A. *and* B.

NEIGHBOUR. What did he give youse?

PRISONER B. [*passing into cell*]. Extra six ounces of bread. Says we're undernourished.

PRISONER A. Is the bar open yet?

NEIGHBOUR. Never you mind the bar. I've cruel pains in my leg that I want rubbed to take out the rheumatics, not to be jeered at, and I've had them genuine since the war.

PRISONER A. What war? The economic war?

NEIGHBOUR. Ah, you maggot. It's all your fault, Dunlavin, telling them fellows we do get an odd sup out of the spirit bottle. Letting everyone know our business.

PRISONERS A. *and* B. *go into cells and shut the doors.*

DUNLAVIN. No sign of Holy Healey yet.

NEIGHBOUR. You're wasting your time chasing after old Healey. He told me here one day, and I trying to get myself an old overcoat out of him, that he was here only as a head man of the Department of Justice, and he couldn't do other business of any other sort or size whatever, good, bad or indifferent. It's my opinion that old Healey does be half-jarred a deal of the time anyway.

DUNLAVIN. The likes of Healey would take a sup all right, but being a high-up civil servant, he wouldn't drink under his own name. You'd see the likes of Healey nourishing themselves with balls of malt, at eleven in the morning, in little back snugs round Merrion Row. The barman would lose his job if he so much as breathed their name. It'd be "Mr. H. wants a drop of water but not too much." "Yes, Mr. O." "No, sir, Mr. Mac wasn't in this morning." "Yes, Mr. D. Fine morning; it will be a lovely day if it doesn't snow." Educated drinking, you know. Even a bit of chat about God at an odd time, so as you'd think God was in another department, but not long off the Bog, and they was doing Him a good turn to be talking well about Him.

NEIGHBOUR. Here's the other two back. The M.O. will be down to us soon.

LIFER *and* OTHER FELLOW *go into cells and shut the doors.*

DUNLAVIN. That other fellow's not looking as if this place is agreeing with him.

NEIGHBOUR. You told me a minute ago that I wasn't even to speak to him.

DUNLAVIN. Ah, when all is said and done, he's someone's rearing after all, he could be worse, he could be a screw or an official from the Department.

WARDER REGAN *comes on with a bottle marked "methylated spirit".*

WARDER REGAN. You're the two for rubs, for your rheumatism.

DUNLAVIN. That's right, Mr. Regan sir, old and bet, sir, that's us. And the old pains is very bad with us these times, sir.

WARDER REGAN. Not so much lip, and sit down whoever is first for treatment.

DUNLAVIN. That's me, sir. Age before ignorance, as the man said. [*Sits in the chair.*]

WARDER REGAN. Rise the leg of your trousers. Which leg is it?

DUNLAVIN. The left, sir.

WARDER REGAN. That's the right leg you're showing me

DUNLAVIN. That's what I was saying, sir. The left is worst one day and the right is bad the next. To be on the safe side, you'd have to do two of them. It's only the mercy of God I'm not a centipede, sir, with the weather that's in it.

WARDER REGAN. Is that where the pain is?

DUNLAVIN [*bending down slowly towards the bottle*]. A little lower down, sir, if you please. [*Grabs the bottle and raises it to his mouth.*] Just a little lower down, sir, if it's all equal to you.

REGAN *rubs, head well bent, and* DUNLAVIN *drinks long and deeply and as quickly lowers the bottle on to the floor again, wiping his mouth and making the most frightful grimaces, for the stuff doesn't go down easy at first. He goes through the pantomime of being burnt inside for* NEIGHBOUR'S *benefit and rubs his mouth with the back of his hand.*

DUNLAVIN. Ah, that's massive, sir. 'Tis you that has the healing hand. You must have desperate luck at the horses; I'd only love to be with you copying your dockets. [REGAN *turns and pours more spirit on his hands.*] Ah, that's it, sir, well into me I can feel it going. [*Reaches forward towards the bottle again, drinks.*] Ah, that's it, I can feel it going right into me. And doing me all the good in the world. [REGAN *reaches and puts more spirit on his hand and sets to rubbing again.*] That's it, sir, thorough does it; if you're going to do a thing at all you might as well do it well. [*Reaches forward for the bottle again and raises it.* NEIGHBOUR *looks across in piteous appeal to him not to drink so much, but he merely waves the bottle in elegant salute, as if to wish him good health, and takes another drink.*] May God reward you, sir, you must be the seventh son of the seventh son or one of the Lees from Limerick on your mother's side maybe. [*Drinks again.*] Ah, that's the cure for the cold of the wind and the world's neglectment.

WARDER REGAN. Right, now you.

NEIGHBOUR *comes forward.*

WARDER DONELLY (*offstage*]. All present and correct, Mr. Healey, sir.

DUNLAVIN. Holy Healey!

Enter WARDER DONELLY.

WARDER DONELLY. This way, Mr. Healey.

WARDER REGAN. Attention! Stand by your doors.

DUNLAVIN. By the left, laugh.

WARDER DONELLY. This way.

Enter MR. HEALEY, *an elegantly dressed gentleman.*

HEALEY. Good morning.

WARDER DONELLY. Any complaints?

PRISONER A. No, sir.

HEALEY. Good morning!

WARDER DONELLY. Any complaints?

OTHER FELLOW.
PRISONER B. } No, sir.

HEALEY. Good morning all! Well, now, I'm here representing the Department of Justice, if there are any complaints now is the time to make them.

SEVERAL PRISONERS. No complaints, sir.

WARDEN REGAN. All correct, sir. Two receiving medical treatment here, sir.

DUNLAVIN. Just getting the old leg rubbed, sir, Mr. Healey.

HEALEY. Well, well, it almost smells like a bar.

DUNLAVIN. I'm near drunk myself on the smell of it, sir.

HEALEY. Don't let me interrupt the good work.

DUNLAVIN. Ah, the old legs. It's being out in all weathers that does it, sir. Of course we don't have that to contend with while we're here, sir.

HEALEY. Out in all weathers, I should think not indeed. Well, my man, I will be inspecting your cell amongst others in due course.

DUNLAVIN. Yes, sir.

HEALEY. It's always a credit to you, I must say that. [*He turns to* REGAN.] Incorrigible, some of these old fellows, but rather amusing.

WARDER REGAN. Yes, sir.

HEALEY. It's Regan, isn't it?

WARDER REGAN. Yes, sir.

HEALEY. Ah yes, you're helping the Canon at the execution tomorrow morning, I understand.

WARDER REGAN. Well, I shall be with the condemned man sir, seeing that he doesn't do away with himself during the night and that he goes down the hole with his neck properly broken in the morning, without making too much fuss about it.

HEALEY. A sad duty.

WARDER REGAN. Neck breaking and throttling, sir? [HEALEY *gives him a sharp look.*] You must excuse me, sir. I've seen rather a lot of it. They say familiarity breeds contempt.

HEALEY. Well, we have one consolation, Regan, the condemned man gets the priest and the sacraments, more than his victim got maybe. I venture to suggest that some of them die holier deaths than if they had finished their natural span.

WARDER REGAN. We can't advertise "Commit a murder and die a happy death," sir. We'd have them all at it. They take religion very seriously in this country.

HEALEY. Quite, quite so! Now, I understand you have the reprieved man over here, Regan.

WARDER REGAN. No. twenty-six sir.

DUNLAVIN. Just beside me, sir.

HEALEY. Ah, yes! So here we are! Here's the lucky man, eh? Well, now, the Governor will explain your position to you later in the day. Your case will be examined every five years. Meanwhile I thought you might like a holy picture to hang up in your cell. Keep a cheerful countenance, my friend. God gave you back your life and the least you can do is to thank him with every breath you draw! Right? Well, be of good heart. I will call in and see you again, that is, if duty permits. [He *moves to* DUNLAVIN'S *cell.*]

HEALEY [*at* DUNLAVIN'S *cell*]. Very creditable. Hm.

DUNLAVIN. Well, to tell you the truth, sir, it's a bit extra special today. You see, we heard you was here.

HEALEY. Very nice.

DUNLAVIN. Of course I do like to keep my little place as homely as I can with the little holy pictures you gave me of Blessed Martin, sir.

HEALEY. I see you don't recognize the colour bar.

DUNLAVIN. The only bar I recognize, sir, is the Bridge Bar or the Beamish House the corner of Thomas Street.

HEALEY. Well, I must be off now, and I'm glad to see you're being well looked after.

DUNLAVIN. It's neither this nor that, but if you could spare a minute, sir?

HEALEY. Yes, what is it? But hurry; remember I've a lot to do today.

DUNLAVIN. It's like this, sir. I won't always be here, sir, having me leg rubbed and me bit of grub brought to me.

As it says in the Bible, sir, have it yourself or be without it and put ye by for the rainy day, for thou knowest not the night thou mayest be sleeping in a lobby.

HEALEY. Yes, yes, but what is it you want?

DUNLAVIN. I've the chance of a little room up round Buckingham Street, sir, if you could only give me a letter to the Room-Keepers after I go out, for a bit of help with the rent.

HEALEY. Well, you know, when I visit the prison, I'm not here as a member of any outside organization of which I may be a member but simply as an official of the Department of Justice.

DUNLAVIN. Yes, but where else would I be likely to meet you, sir? I'd hardly bump into you in the Bridge Bar when I'd be outside, would I, sir?

HEALEY. No, no, certainly not. But you know the Society offices in the Square. See me there any Friday night, between eight and nine.

DUNLAVIN. Thank you, sir, and a bed in heaven to you, sir.

HEALEY. And the same to you. [*Goes to next cell.*]

DUNLAVIN. And many of them, and I hope we're all here this time next year [*venomously after* MR. HEALEY] that it may choke you.

WARDER DONELLY *bangs on* LIFER'S *closed door, then looks in.*

WARDER DONELLY. Jesus Christ, sir. He's put the sheet up! Quick.

REGAN *and* DONELLY *go into* LIFER'S *cell. He is hanging. They cut him down.*

WARDER REGAN. Gently does it.

They lay him down in the passage and try to restore him.

HEALEY. What a dreadful business, and with this other coming off tomorrow.

THE PRISONERS *crowd out of line.*

WARDER DONELLY. Get back to your cells!

HEALEY. Is he still with us?

WARDER REGAN. He'll be all right in an hour or two. Better get the M.O., Mr. Donelly.

The triangle sounds.

WARDER DONELLY. B. Wing, two, three and one. Stand by your doors. Right, lead on. Now come on, come on, this is no holiday. Right sir, over to you. Lead on, B.1.

WARDER REGAN *and* HEALEY *are left with the unconscious* LIFER.

HEALEY. Dear, dear. The Canon will be very upset about this.

WARDER REGAN. There's not much harm done, thank God. They don't have to put a death certificate against the receipt for his live body.

HEALEY. That doesn't seem a very nice way of looking at it, Regan.

WARDER REGAN. A lot of people mightn't consider ours a very nice job, sir.

HEALEY. Ours?

WARDER REGAN. Yes, ours, sir. Mine, the Canon's, the hangman's, and if you don't mind my saying so, yours, sir.

HEALEY. Society cannot exist without prisons, Regan. My

job is to bring what help and comfort I can to these unfortunates. Really, a man with your outlook, I cannot see why you stay in the service.

WARDER REGAN. It's a soft job, sir, between hangings.

The triangle is heard. The M.O. *comes on with two stretcher-bearers.*

The curtain falls.

ACT II

The curtain rises

The prison yard, a fine evening.

VOICE OF PRISONER [*off-stage, singing*].

A hungry feeling came o'er me stealing
And the mice were squealing in my prison cell
And the old triangle
Went jingle jangle
Along the banks of the Royal Canal.

WARDER DONELLY. B.1. B.2. B.3. Head on for exercise, right! Lead on, B.1. All one, away to exercise.

The prisoners file out, WARDER DONELLY *with them.*

On a fine spring evening,
The lag lay dreaming
The seagulls wheeling high above the wall,
And the old triangle
Went jingle jangle
Along the banks of the Royal Canal.
The screw was peeping
The lag was sleeping,

The prisoners wander where they will; most go and take a glance at the half-dug grave.

While he lay weeping for the girl Sal,

WARDER DONELLY. Who's the bloody baritone? Shut up that noise, you. Where do you think you are?

NEIGHBOUR. It's not up here, sir; it's one of the fellows in the basement, sir, in the solitary.

WARDER DONELLY. He must be getting birdseed with his bread and water. I'll bloody well show him he's not in a singing house. [*Song is still going on.*] Hey, shut up that noise! Shut up there or I'll leave you weeping. Where do you think you are? [*Song stops.*] You can get sitting down any of you that wants it. [DUNLAVIN *sits.*]

NEIGHBOUR [*at the grave*]. They'll have to bottom out another couple of feet before morning.

PRISONER B. They! Us you mean; they've got four of us in a working party after tea.

NEIGHBOUR. You want to get that clay nice and neat for filling in. [*He spits and wanders away.*]

PRISONER B. We'll get a couple of smokes for the job at least.

They wander.

NEIGHBOUR. How are you, Neighbour?

DUNLAVIN. Dying.

NEIGHBOUR. If you are itself, it's greed that's killing you. I only got a sup of what was left.

DUNLAVIN. I saved your life then; it was very bad meths.

PRISONER B. What did Regan say when he caught youse lying in the cell?

NEIGHBOUR. He wanted to take us up for drinking it on him, but Dunlavin said we were distracted with the events of the morning and didn't know what we were doing. So he just told us to get to hell out of it and he hoped it would destroy us for life.

DUNLAVIN. May God forgive him.

NEIGHBOUR. I thought it was as good a drop of meths as ever I tasted. It would never come up to the pre-war article, but between the spring-time and the warmth of it, it would put new life into you. Oh, it's a grand evening and another day's work behind us.

PRISONER B. With the winter over, Neighbour, I suppose you don't feel a day over ninety.

NEIGHBOUR. If you'd have done all the time I have you wouldn't look so young.

PRISONER A. What time? Sure, you never done a lagging in your life. A month here and a week there for lifting the collection box out of a chapel or running out of a chemist's with a bottle of cheap wine. Anything over six months would be the death of you.

NEIGHBOUR. Oh, you're the hard chaw.

PRISONER A. Two laggings, I've done. Five year and seven, and a bit of Preventive Detention, on the Moor and at Parkhurst.

NEIGHBOUR. What for? Ferocious begging?

PRISONER A. I've never been a grasshopper or a nark for the screws anyway, wherever I was; and if you were in a lagging station I know what they'd give you, shopping the poor bastard that was singing in the chokey. He was only trying to be company for himself down there all alone and not knowing whether it was day or night.

NEIGHBOUR. I only did it for his own good. If the screw hadn't checked him the Principal might have been coming out and giving him an extra few days down there.

DUNLAVIN. Will youse give over the pair of youse for God's sake. The noise of youse battering me bared nerves is unhuman. Begod, an Englishman would have more nature to a fellow lying with a sick head. A methylated martyr, that's what I am.

NEIGHBOUR [*to* PRISONER A.]. Meself and that man sitting there, we done time before you came up. In Kilmainham, and that's where you never were. First fourteen days without a mattress, skilly three times a day. None of your sitting out in the yard like nowadays. I got my toe amputated by one of the old lags so I could get into hospital for a feed.

DUNLAVIN [*looks up and feebly moans*]. A pity you didn't get your head amputated as you were at it. It would have kept you quiet for a bit.

NEIGHBOUR. I got me mouth to talk, the same as the next man. Maybe we're not all that well up, that we get up at the Christmas concert and do the electrocutionist performance, like some I could mention.

DUNLAVIN. It's neither this nor that, Neighbour, but if you would only give over arguing the toss about nothing and change over to a friendly subject of mutual interest—like the quare fellow that's to be topped in the morning.

NEIGHBOUR. True, true, Dunlavin, and a comfortable old flowery dell he'll have down there. (He *prods the grave with his stick*.] We'll be eating the cabbages off that one in a month or two.

PRISONER A. You're in a terrible hurry to get the poor scut under the cabbages. How do you know he won't get a reprieve, like old Silver-top?

LIFER. Jesus, Mary and Joseph, you'd like to see me in there, wouldn't you! [*He moves violently away from them.*]

NEIGHBOUR. Your man doesn't like any talk about hanging.

PRISONER A. No more would you, if you'd tried to top yourself this morning.

NEIGHBOUR. Anyway he's gone now and we can have a chat about it in peace. Sure we must be saying something and it's better than scandalizing our neighbours.

PRISONER B. You never know what might happen to the quare fellow. God is good.

PRISONER C. And has a good mother.

They look in surprise at the young person who has quietly joined them.

DUNLAVIN. No, no, it's too late now for him to be chucked.

PRISONER A. It has been known, a last-minute reprieve, you know.

NEIGHBOUR. He bled his brother into a crock, didn't he, that had been set aside for the pig-slaughtering and mangled the remains beyond all hope of identification.

PRISONER C. Go bfoiridh Dia reinn.

NEIGHBOUR. He hasn't got a chance, never in a race of cats. He'll be hung as high as Guilderoy.

PRISONER A. You're the life of the party, aren't you? You put me in mind of the little girl who was sent in to cheer her father up. She was so good at it that he cut his throat.

PRISONER E. Ah, sure he was only computing the odds to it. He'll be topped.

NEIGHBOUR. I'd lay me Sunday bacon on it if anyone would be idiot enough to take me up.

PRISONER E, *a bookie, has been listening.*

PRISONER E. I wouldn't take your bacon, but I'll lay it off for you if you like.

Another prisoner watches for the screws. PRISONER E. *acts as if he were a tick-tack man at the races.*

PRISONER E. The old firm. Here we are again. Neighbour lays his Sunday bacon the quare fellow will be topped tomorrow morning. Any takers?

PRISONER D. Five snout.

PRISONER E. Away home to your mother.

MICKSER. Half a bacon.

PRISONER E. Half a . . .

NEIGHBOUR. Even bacons.

PRISONER E. Even bacons. Even bacons any takers? Yourself, sir, come on now, you look like a sportsman.

PRISONER A. I wouldn't eat anything after he'd touched it, not if I were starving.

NEIGHBOUR. Is that so . . .

PRISONER E. Now, now, now, don't interrupt the betting. Any takers?

DUNLAVIN. I'll take him up if only to shut his greedy gob.

NEIGHBOUR. You won't! You're having me on!

DUNLAVIN. No, I'll bet you my Sunday bacon that a reprieve will come through before morning. I feel it in my bones.

NEIGHBOUR. That's the rheumatics.

PRISONER E. Is he on, Neighbour?

NEIGHBOUR. He is.

PRISONER E. Shake on it, the two of youse!

DUNLAVIN. How d'ye do, Lord Lonsdale!

NEIGHBOUR. Never mind all that. The minute the trap goes down tomorrow morning your Sunday bacon is mine.

PRISONER A. God leave you health to enjoy it.

NEIGHBOUR. He'll be topped all right.

PRISONER A. And if he isn't, I'm the very man will tell him you bet your bacon on his life.

NEIGHBOUR. You never would.

PRISONER A. Wouldn't I?

NEIGHBOUR. You'd never be bad enough.

PRISONER A. And what would be bad about it?

NEIGHBOUR. Causing a dissension and a disturbance.

The two YOUNG PRISONERS *enter.*

PRISONER A. You mean he mightn't take it for a joke.

PRISONER B. Here's them two young prisoners; they've the life of Reilly, rambling round the place. Where youse wandering off to now?

SCHOLARA. We came over here to see a chiner of ours. He turned twenty the day before yesterday, so they shifted him away from the Juveniles to here. [*He sees* PRISONER C.] Ah, there you are. We were over in the hospital being examined for going out on Saturday and we had a bit of snout to give you. [*Takes out a Woodbine package, extracts a cigarette from it and gives it to* PRISONER C., *who shyly stands and takes it.*]

PRISONER C. [*quietly*]. Thanks.

SCHOLARA. Gurra morra gut, you mean.

PRISONER C. [*smiles faintly*]. Go raibh maith agat.

SCHOLARA [*grandly*]. Na bac leis. [*To the other prisoners.*] Talks Irish to beat the band. Comes from an island between here and America. And Shaybo will give you a couple of strikers.

SHAYBO [*reaches in the seams of his coat and takes out a match which he presents to* PRISONER C.]. Here you are. It's a bloody shame to shove you over here among all these old men even if you are twenty itself, but maybe you won't be long after us, and you going home.

PRISONER C. [*Kerry accent*]. I will, please God. It will be summer-time and where I come from is lovely when the sun is shining.

[*They stand there, looking embarrassed for a moment.*]

DUNLAVIN. Go on, why don't you kiss him good-bye.

SHAYBO. Eh, Schol, let's have a pike at the grave before the screw comes out.

SCHOLARA. Ah, yes, we must have a look at the grave.

They dive into the grave, the old men shout at them, but WARDER DONELLY *comes to the door of the hospital.*

WARDER DONELLY. Get up to hell out of that and back to your own wing, youse two. [*Shouts to the warders in the prison wing.*] Two on you there, pass them fellows into the Juveniles. Get to hell out of that!

SCHOLARA *and* SHAYBO *samba off, give the so-called V-sign, slap the right biceps with the left palm, and turning lightly, run in through the door.*

NEIGHBOUR. Aren't they the impudent pups? Too easy a time they have of it. I'd tan their pink backsides for them. That'd leave them fresh and easy. Impudent young curs is going these days. No respect for God nor man, pinch anything that wasn't nailed down.

PRISONER B. Neighbour, the meths is rising in you.

DUNLAVIN. He might as well rave there as in bed.

ENGLISH VOICE [*from one of the cell windows*]. I say, I say, down there in the yard.

DUNLAVIN. The voice of the Lord!

PRISONER A. That's the geezer from London that's in over the car smuggling.

ENGLISH VOICE. I say, down there.

PRISONER B. Hello, up there.

NEIGHBOUR. How are you fixed for fillet?

PRISONER B. Shut up a minute. Wait till we hear what is it he wants.

ENGLISH VOICE. Is there any bloke down there going out this week?

PRISONER B. Mickser is going out tomorrow. He's on this exercise. [*Shouts.*] Hold on a minute. [*Looks round.*] Hey, Mickser.

MICKSER. What's up?

PRISONER B. That English fellow that's on remand over the cars, he wants to know if there's anyone going out this week. You're going out tomorrow, ain't you?

MICKSER. Yes, I am. I'm going out in the morning. [*To* ENGLISH PRISONER.] What do you want?

ENGLISH VOICE. I want you to go up and contact my mate. He's in Dublin. It's about bail for me. I can write his name and address here and let it down to you on my string. I didn't want the law to get his address in Dublin, so I can't write to him. I got a quid in with me, without the screw finding it, and I'll let it down with the address if you'll do it.

MICKSER. Good enough. Let down the address and the quid.

ENGLISH VOICE. My mate will give you some more when you see him.

MICKSER. That's all right. Let the quid down now and the address before the screw comes out of the hospital. I'm going out tomorrow and I'll see him for you, soon as we get out of the market pubs at half two.

PRISONER B. He's letting it down now.

MICKSER. There's the quid anyway. [*Reading the note.* NEIGHBOUR *gets to his feet and goes behind and peers over his shoulder.* MICKSER *sees him.*] Get to hell out of it, you.

NEIGHBOUR. I only just wanted to have a look at what he wrote.

MICKSER. And have his mate in the Bridewell, before the day was out. I know you, you bloody old stag.

NEIGHBOUR. I saw the day you wouldn't say the like of that.

MICKSER [*proffering him the pound*]. Here, get a mass said for yourself.

NEIGHBOUR. It wouldn't do you much harm to put yourself under the hand of a priest either.

MICKSER [*laughs at him*]. That's for sinners. Only dirty people has to wash.

NEIGHBOUR. A man of your talent and wasting your time here.

MICKSER [*going back to walk with the prisoners behind*]. Good luck now, Neighbour. I'll call up and see you in the hospice for the dying.

NEIGHBOUR [*stands and calls loudly after him*]. You watch yourself. I saw the quare fellow in here a couple of years ago. He was a young hard chaw like you in all the pride of his strength and impudence. He was kicking a ball about over in A yard and I was walking around with poor old Mockridge, neither of us minding no one. All of a sudden I gets such a wallop on the head it knocks the legs from under me and very nigh cuts off my ear. "You headed that well", says he, and I deaf for three days after it! Who's got the best of it now, young as he is and strong as he is? How will his own ear feel tomorrow morning, with the washer under it, and whose legs will be the weakest when the trap goes down and he's slung into the pit? And what use is the young heart?

Some of the prisoners walking round stop and listen to him, but MICKSER *gives him a contemptuous look and walks on, shouting at him in passing.*

MICKSER. Get along with you, you dirty half animal.

A WARDER *passes, sounds of the town heard, factory sirens, distant ships. Some of the prisoners pace up and down like caged animals.*

NEIGHBOUR. Dunlavin, have you the loan of a pencil for a minute?

DUNLAVIN. What do you want it for?

NEIGHBOUR. I just want to write something to that English fellow about his bail.

DUNLAVIN. You'd better hurry, before the screw comes back out.

NEIGHBOUR *writes.*

NEIGHBOUR. Hey, you up there that's looking for the bail.

ENGLISH VOICE. Hello, you got the quid and the address?

PRISONER A. What's the old dog up to?

DUNLAVIN. Ah, leave him alone. He's a bit hasty, but poor old Neighbour has good turns in him.

PRISONER A. So has a corkscrew.

NEIGHBOUR. Let down your string and I'll send you up this bit of a message.

ENGLISH VOICE [*his hands can be seen at the window holding the note*]. "Get a bucket and bail yourself out." [*Shouts in rage.*] You dirty bastard bleeder to take my quid and I'll tell the bloody screw I will; I'll shop you, you bleeding . . .

MICKSER. What's up with you?

NEIGHBOUR. Get a bucket and bail yourself out. [*Laughing an old man's cackle.*]

ENGLISH VOICE. You told me to get a bucket and bail my bleeding self out, but I'll tell the screw; I'll shop you about that quid.

MICKSER [*shouts up to the window*] Shut your bloody big mouth for a minute. I told you nothing.

PRISONER A. It was this old get here.

MICKSER. I sent you no message; it was this old pox bottle.

NEIGHBOUR [*ceases to laugh, is alarmed at the approach of* MICKSER]. Now, now, Mickser, take a joke, can't you, it was only a bit of gas.

MICKSER [*advancing*]. I'll give you gas.

(MICKSER *advances on* NEIGHBOUR. *The lags stop and look—suddenly* MICKSER *seizes the old man and, yelling with delight, carries* NEIGHBOUR *over to the grave and thrusts him into it. The prisoners all crowd around kicking dirt on to the old man and shouting "Get a bucket and bail yourself out"*.

PRISONER B. Nick, Mickser, nick, nick, here's the screw.

PRISONER A. It's only the cook with the quare fellow's tea.

A PRISONER *comes through the hospital gate and down the steps. He wears a white apron, carries a tray and is surrounded by an interested band, except for the* LIFER, *who stands apart, and* DUNLAVIN, *who lies prone on the front asleep. From the prisoners around the food rises an excited chorus:*

PRISONER A. Rashers and eggs.

PRISONER B. He got that last night.

MICKSER. Chicken.

NEIGHBOUR. He had that for dinner.

PRISONER B. Sweet cake.

PRISONER A. It's getting hung he is, not married.

NEIGHBOUR. Steak and onions.

MICKSER. Sausages and bacon.

PRISONER B. And liver.

PRISONER A. Pork chops.

PRISONER B. Pig's feet.

PRISONER A. Salmon.

NEIGHBOUR. Fish and chips.

MICKSER. Jelly and custard.

NEIGHBOUR. Roast lamb.

PRISONER A. Plum pudding.

PRISONER B. Turkey.

NEIGHBOUR. Goose.

PRISONERS A., B., AND NEIGHBOUR. Rashers and eggs.

ALL. Rashers and eggs, rashers and eggs, and eggs and rashers and eggs and rashers it is.

COOK [*desperate*]. Ah, here, lads.

PRISONERS. Here, give us a look, lift up the lid, eh, here, I never seen it.

The COOK *struggles to protect his cargo, the* PRISONERS *mill round in a loose scrum of excitement and greed, their nostrils mad almost to the point of snatching a bit. There is a roar from the gate.*

WARDER DONELLY [*from inside the hospital gate*]. Get to hell out of that. What do youse think you are on?

The PRISONERS *scatter in a rush.*

The COOK *with great dignity carries on.*

NEIGHBOUR [*sitting down*]. Oh, the two eggs, the yolk in the middle like . . . a bride's eye under a pink veil, and the grease of the rashers . . . pale and pure like melted gold.

DUNLAVIN. Oh, may God forgive you, as if a body wasn't sick enough as it is.

NEIGHBOUR. And the two big back rashers.

PRISONER A. Go along, you begrudging old dog. Maybe when you go back the standard of living in your town residence, No. 1 St. James Street, might be gone up. And they'll be serving rashers and eggs. You'd do a lot for them, when you'd begrudge them to a man for his last meal on this earth.

NEIGHBOUR. Well, it's not his last meal if you want to know. He'll get a supper tonight and a breakfast in the morning, and I don't begrudge him the little he'll eat of that, seeing the rope stew to follow, and lever pudding and trap door doddle for desert. And anyway didn't you run over the same as the rest of us to see what he was getting?

PRISONER A. And if I did, it wasn't to begrudge it to the man.

PRISONER B. Sure we all ran over, anything to break the monotony in a kip like this.

The triangle is heard.

PRISONER A. [*gloomily*]. I suppose you're right. In Strangeways, Manchester, and I in it during the war, we used to wish for an air-raid. We had one and we were left locked up in our cells. We stood up on our tables and took the blackouts off the windows and had a grand-stand view of the whole city burning away under us. The screws were running round shouting in the spy-holes at us to get down from the windows, but they soon ran off down the shelters. We had a great view of the whole thing till a bomb landed on the Assize Court next door, and the blast killed twenty of the lags. They were left standing on their tables without a mark on them, stone dead. Sure anyway, we all agreed it broke the monotony.

Enter WARDER DONELLY.

WARDER DONELLY. Right, fall in there!

PRISONER B. Don't forget the bet, Neighbour.

WARDER DONELLY. Come on, get in line there.

PRISONER A. And don't forget what I'm going to tell the quare fellow.

WARDER DONELLY. Silence there. [*Search begins.*] What's this you've got in your pocket? A file? Scissors out of the bag shop? No? A bit of rope? Oh, your handkerchief, so it is. [*Searching next* PRISONER.] You here, what's this? A bit of wax end, you forgot to leave in the bag shop? Well, don't forget the next time. What's this? [MAN *takes out two inches of rope.*] What's this for? You were roping mail bags today, and after all they don't rope themselves. Ah, you forgot to leave it behind? Well, go easy, save as much as that each time and in five years' time you'd have enough to make a rope ladder. Oh, you're only doing six months? Well maybe you want to save the taxpayers a few quid and hang yourself. Sorrow the loss if you did, but they'd want to know where you got the rope from. [PRISONERS *laugh as they are expected to do.*] Come on, next man. [*He hurries along now.*] Come along now, no mailbags, scissors, needles, knives, razor blades, guns, hatchets or empty porter bottles. No? [*To the last* PRISONER.] Well, will you buy a ticket to the Police Ball?

PRISONERS *laugh dutifully.*

WARDER REGAN [*voice from prison wing*]. All done, sir?

PRISONER A. Don't forget, Neighbour.

WARDER DONELLY. Right, sir, on to you, sir. [*Gate swings open.*] Right, lead on, B.1.

NEIGHBOUR. Anyway, his grave's dug and the hangman's on his way.

PRISONER A. That doesn't mean a thing, they always dig the grave, just to put the wind up them—

WARDER DONELLY. Silence!

The prisoners march, the gate clangs behind them; the tramp of their feet is heard as they mark time inside.

WARDER REGAN [*voice from the prison wing*]. Right, B. Wing, bang out your doors. B.1, get in off your steps and bang out your doors, into your cells and bang out your doors. Get locked up. BANG THEM DOORS! GET INSIDE AND BANG OUT THEM DOORS!

The last door bangs lonely on its own and then there is silence.

VOICE FROM BELOW [*singing*].

> The wind was rising,
> And the day declining
> As I lay pining in my prison cell
> And that old triangle
> Went jingle jangle

The triangle is beaten, the gate of the prison wing opens and the CHIEF *and* WARDER DONELLY *come down the steps and approach the grave.*

> Along the banks of the Royal Canal.

CHIEF [*resplendent in silver braid*]. Who's that singing?

WARDER DONELLY. I think it's one of the prisoners in the chokey, sir.

CHIEF. Where?

WARDER DONELLY. In the punishment cells, sir.

CHIEF. That's more like it. Well, tell him to cut it out.

SONG.

In the female prison
There are seventy women . . .

WARDER DONELLY [*goes down to the area and leans and shouts*]. Hey, you down there, cut it out, or I'll give you jingle jangle.

The song stops. WARDER DONELLY *walks back.*

CHIEF. Is the quare fellow finished his tea?

WARDER DONELLY. He is. He is just ready to come out for exercise, now. The wings are all clear. They're locked up having their tea. He'll be along any minute.

CHIEF. He's coming out here?

WARDER DONELLY. Yes, sir.

CHIEF [*exasperated*]. Do you want him to see his grave, bloody well half dug? Run in quick and tell those bloody idiots to take him out the side door, and exercise him over the far side of the stokehold, and tell them to keep him well into the wall where he'll be out of sight of the cell windows. Hurry and don't let him hear you. Let on it's something about another duty. Warders! You'd get better in Woolworths.

He goes to the area and shouts down.

Hey, you down there. You in the cell under the steps. You do be singing there to keep yourself company? You needn't be afraid, it's only the Chief. How long you doing down there? Seven days No. 1 and twenty-one days No. 2. God bless us and love us, you must have done something desperate. I may be able to do something for you, though God knows you needn't count on it, I don't own the place. You what? With who? Ah sure, I often have a bit of a tiff with the same man myself. We'll see what we can do for you. It's a long time to be stuck down there, no matter who you had the tiff with.

Enter WARDER DONELLY.

CHIEF. Well?

WARDER DONELLY. It's all right, they've brought him out the other way.

They look out beyond the stage.

CHIEF. Looks as if they're arguing the toss about something.

WARDER DONELLY. Football.

CHIEF. Begod, look at them stopping while the quare fellow hammers his point home.

WARDER DONELLY. I was down in the condemned cell while he was getting his tea. I asked him if it was all right. He said it was, and "Aren't the evenings getting a grand stretch?" he says.

CHIEF. Look at him now, putting his nose to the air.

WARDER DONELLY. He's a grand evening for his last.

CHIEF. I took the name of the fellow giving the concert in the punishment cells. In the morning when we get this over, see he's shifted to Hell's gates over the far side. He can serenade the stokehold wall for a change if he's light enough to make out his music.

WARDER DONELLY *copies the name and number.*

CHIEF. I have to attend to every mortal thing in this place. None of youse seem to want to do a hand's turn, bar draw your money—you're quick enough at that. Well, come on, let's get down to business.

WARDER DONELLY *goes and uncovers the grave.*

CHIEF [*looking off*]. Just a minute. It's all right. They've taken him round the back of the stokehold. [*Looking at the grave.*] Not so bad, another couple of feet out of the bottom and we're elected. Regan should be down with the working party any minute, as soon as the quare fellow's finished his exercise.

WARDER DONELLY. There, he's away in now, sir. See him looking at the sky?

CHIEF. You'd think he was trying to kiss it good-bye. Well, that's the last he'll see of it.

WARDER DONELLY. No chance of a reprieve, sir?

CHIEF. Not a chance. Healey never even mentioned fixing up a line with the Post Office. If there'd been any chance of developments he'd have asked us to put a man on all night. All he said was "The Governor will get the last word before the night's out." That means only one thing. Go ahead.

WARDERS REGAN *and* CRIMMIN *come out with* PRISONERS A. B. C. *and* D.

WARDER REGAN. Working party all correct, sir. Come on, get those boards off. Bottom out a couple more feet and leave the clay at the top, nice and neat.

CHIEF. Oh, Mr. Regan.

WARDER REGAN. Take over, Mr. Crimmin.

CHIEF. Mr. Regan. All I was going to say was—why don't

you take yourself a bit of a rest while these fellows are at work on the grave. It's a long old pull till eight to-morrow morning.

WARDER REGAN. Thank you, sir.

CHIEF. Don't mention it. I'll see you before you go down to the cell. Get yourself a bit of a smoke, in the hospital. Don't forget now.

He *and* WARDER DONELLY *go back in.*

WARDER REGAN. Mr. Crimmin. The Chief, a decent man, he's after giving us his kind permission to go into hospital and have a sit down and a smoke for ourselves when these fellows have the work started. He knew we'd go in any-way, so he saw the chance of being floochalach, at no expense to the management. Here [*Takes out a packet of cigarettes, and takes some from it.*], here's a few fags for the lads.

CRIMMIN. I'll give them some of mine too.

WARDER REGAN. Don't do anything of the sort. One each is enough, you can slip them a couple when they're going to be locked up, if you like, but if these fellows had two fags each, they'd not work at all but spend the time out here blowing smoke rings in the evening air like lords. I'll slip in now, you come in after me. Tell them not to have them in their mouths if the Chief or the Governor comes out.

He goes up the steps to the hospital.

CRIMMIN [*calls* PRISONER C.) Hey!

PRISONER C. [*comes to him*]. Seadh a Thomais?

CRIMMIN [*gives him cigarettes and matches*]. Seo, cupla toitin. Taim f hein is an screw eile ag did isteach chiung an oispeasdal, noimest Roinn amach no toitini siud, is glacfaidh sibh gal, M. thagann an Governor nor Chief, no an Principal, no blodh in bhur mbeil agaib iad. A' tuigeann tu?

PRISONER C. Tuigim, a Thomais, go raidh maith agat.

CRIMMIN [*officially*]. Right, now get back to your work.

PRISONER C. Yes, sir.

CRIMMIN *goes up the hospital steps.*

PRISONER C. He gave me some cigarettes.

PRISONER D. *has gone straight to the grave,* PRISONER B. *is near it.*

PRISONER A. May I never dig a grave for less! You two get on and do a bit of digging while we have a quiet burn, then we'll take over.

PRISONER C. He said to watch out for the chief and them.

PRISONER B. Pass down a light to your man. He says he'd enjoy it better down there, where he can't be seen! Decent of him and Regan wasn't it?

PRISONER A. They'd have you dead from decency. That same Regan was like a savage in the bag shop today, you couldn't get a word to the fellow next to you.

PRISONER C. I never saw him like that before.

PRISONER B. He's always the same at a time like this, hanging seems to get on his nerves.

PRISONER A. Why should he worry, he won't feel it.

PRISONER B. He's on the last watch. Twelve till eight.

PRISONER A. Till death do us part.

PRISONER C. The quare fellow asked for him, didn't he?

PRISONER A. They all do.

PRISONER C. He asked to have Mr. Crimmin too.

PRISONER A. It'll break that young screw up, and him only a wet day in the place.

PRISONER B. Funny the way they all ask for Regan. Perhaps they think he'll bring them good luck, him being good living.

PRISONER A. Good living! Whoever heard of a good living screw? Did you never hear of the screw, married the prostitute?

PRISONER B. No, what happened to him?

PRISONER A. He dragged her down to his own level.

PRISONER B. He told me once that if I kept off the beer I need never come back here. I asked him what about himself, and he told me he was terrible hardened to it and would I pray for him.

PRISONER C. When I was over in the Juveniles he used to talk like that to us. He said that the Blessed Virgin knew us better than the police or the judges—or ourselves even. We might think we were terrible sinners but she knew we were good boys only a bit wild . . .

PRISONER A. Bloody mad he is.

PRISONER C. And that we were doing penance here for the men who took us up, especially the judges, they being mostly rich old men with great opportunity for vice.

PRISONER D. *appears from the grave.*

PRISONER A. The dead arose and appeared to many.

PRISONER A. *goes and rearranges the work which* PRISONER D. *has upset.*

PRISONER B. What's brought you out of your fox hole?

PRISONER D. I thought it more discreet to remain in concealment while I smoked but I could not stop down there listening to talk like that, as a ratepayer, I couldn't stand for it, especially those libellous remarks about the judiciary.

He looks accusingly at the boy.

PRISONER C. I was only repeating what Mr. Regan said, sir.

PRISONER D. He could be taken up for it. According to that man, there should be no such thing as law and order. We could all be murdered in our beds, the innocent prey of every ruffian that took it into his head to appropriate our goods, our lives even. Property must have security! What do you think society would come to without police and judges and suitable punishments? Chaos! In my opinion hanging's too good for 'em.

PRISONER C. Oh, Mr. Regan doesn't believe in capital punishment, sir.

PRISONER D. My God, the man's an atheist! He should be dismissed from the public service. I shall take it up with the Minister when I get out of here. I went to school with his cousin.

PRISONER A. Who the hell does he think he is, a bloody high court judge?

PRISONER D. Chaos!

PRISONER B. He's in for embezzlement, there were two suicides and a bye-election over him.

PRISONER D. There are still a few of us who care about the state of the country, you know. My family's national tradition goes back to the Land War. Grandfather did four weeks for incitement to mutiny—and we've never looked back since. One of my young nephews, as a matter of fact, has just gone over to Sandhurst.

PRISONER B. Isn't that where you done your four years?

PRISONER A. No, that was Parkhurst.

PRISONER C. [*to others*]. A college educated man in here, funny, isn't it?

PRISONER D. I shall certainly bring all my influence to bear to settle this Regan fellow.

PRISONER C. You must be a very important man, sir.

PRISONER D. I am one of the Cashel Carrolls, my boy, related on my mother's side to the Killens of Killcock.

PRISONER B. Used to wash for our family.

PRISONER C. Go bfoiridh. Dia rainn.

PRISONER D. Irish speaking?

PRISONER C. Yes, sir.

PRISONER D. Then it might interest you to know that I took my gold medal in Irish.

PRISONER C. Does that mean he speaks Irish?

PRISONER D. Of course.

PRISONER C. Oh sir. Ta Caoliumn go leor agamsa. O'n gobliabh an amach, sir.

PRISONER B. That's fixed you.

PRISONER D. Quite. Tuighin thu.

PRISONER B. The young lad's from Kerry, from an island where they don't speak much else.

PRISONER D. Kerry? Well of course you speak with a different dialect to the one I was taught.

PRISONER B. The young screw Crimmin's from the same place. He sneaks up to the landing sometimes when the other screws aren't watching and there they are for hours talking through the spy hole, all in Irish.

PRISONER D. Most irregular.

PRISONER B. There's not much harm in it.

PRISONER D. How can there be proper discipline between warder and prisoner with that kind of familiarity?

PRISONER C. He does only be giving me the news from home and who's gone to America or England; he's not long up here and neither am I . . . the two of us do each be as lonely as the other.

PRISONER B. The lad here sings an old song betimes. It's very nice. It makes the night less lonely, each man alone and sad maybe in the old cell. The quare fellow heard him singing and after he was sentenced to death he sent over word he'd be listening every night around midnight for him.

PRISONER A. You'd better make a bit effort tonight, kid, for his last concert.

PRISONER C. Ah, God help him! Sure, you'd pity him all the same. It must be awful to die at the end of a swinging rope and a black hood over his poor face.

PRISONER A. Begod, he's not being topped for nothing—to cut his own brother up and butcher him like a pig.

PRISONER D. I must heartily agree with you sir, a barbarian if ever there was one.

PRISONER C. Maybe he did those things, but God help him this minute and he knowing this night his last on earth. Waiting over there he is, to be shaken out of his sleep and rushed to the rope.

PRISONER A. What sleep will he take? They won't have to set the alarm clock for a quarter to eight, you can bet your life on that.

PRISONER C. May he find peace on the other side.

PRISONER A. Or his brother waiting to have a word with him about being quartered in such an unmannerly fashion.

PRISONER C. None of us can know for certain.

PRISONER D. It was proved in a court of law that this man had experience as a pork butcher and put his expert knowledge to use by killing his brother with an axe and dismembering the body, the better to dispose of it.

PRISONER C. Go bfoiridh. Dia rainn.

PRISONER A. I wouldn't put much to the court of law part of it, but I heard about it myself from a fellow in from his part of the country. He said he had the brother strung up in an outhouse like a pig.

PRISONER D. Actually he was bleeding him into a farmhouse vessel according to the evidence. He should be hung three or four times over.

PRISONER A. Seeing your uncle was at school with the President's granny, perhaps he could fix it up for you.

PRISONER C. I don't believe he is a bad man. When I was on remand he used to walk around with me at exercise every day and he was sad when I told him about my brother, who died in the Yank's army, and my father, who was buried alive at the demolition of Manchester . . . He was great company for me who knew no one, only jackeens would be making game of me, and I'm sorry for him.

PRISONER A. Sure, it's a terrible pity about you and him. Maybe the jackeens should spread out the red carpet for you and every other bog barbarian that comes into the place.

He moves away irritably.

Let's get a bit more off this bloody hole.

PRISONER B. Nick. Nick.

WARDER REGAN [*entering with* CRIMMIN]. I've been watching you for the last ten minutes and damn the thing you've done except yap, yap, yap the whole time. The

Chief or the Governor or any of them could have been watching you. They'd have thought it was a bloody mothers' meeting. What with you and my other bald mahogany gas pipe here.

PRISONER D. We were merely exchanging a few comments, sir.

WARDER REGAN. That's a lie and it's not worth a lie.

PRISONER A. All right! So we were caught talking at labour. I didn't ask to be an undertaker's assistant. Go on, bang me inside and case me in the morning! Let the Governor give me three days of No. 1.

WARDER REGAN. Much that'd worry you.

PRISONER A. You're dead right.

WARDER REGAN. Don't be such a bloody big baby. We all know you're a hard case. Where did you do your lagging? On the bog?

PRISONER A. I did not. Two laggings I done! At Parkhurst and on the Moor.

WARDER REGAN. There's the national inferiority complex for you. Our own Irish cat-o'-nine-tails and the batons of the warders loaded with lead from Carrick mines aren't good enough for him. He has to go Dartmooring and Parkhursting it. It's a wonder you didn't go further while you were at it, to Sing Sing or Devil's Island.

PRISONER A. [*stung*]. I'm not here to be made a mock of, whether I done a lagging in England or not.

WARDER REGAN. Who said a word about it, only yourself—doing the returned Yank in front of these other fellows? Look, the quare fellow's got to be buried in the morning, whether we like it or not, so cut the mullarkey and get back to work.

PRISONER A. I don't let anyone make game of me!

WARDER REGAN. Well, what are you going to do about it? Complain to Holy Healey's department? He's a fine bloody imposter, isn't he? Like an old I.R.A. man with a good agency in the Sweep now. Recommend me to the respectable people! Drop it for Christ's sake, man. It's a bad night for all of us. Fine job, isn't it, for a young fellow like him, fresh from his mother's apron strings. You haven't forgotten what it's like to come from a decent home, have you, with the family rosary said every night?

PRISONER A. I haven't any time for that kind of gab. I never saw religion do anything but back up the screws. I was in Walton last Christmas Eve, when the clergyman came to visit a young lad that had been given eighteen strokes of the cat that morning. When the kid stopped moaning long enough to hear what he had to say, he was told to think on the Lord's sufferings, then the cell door closed with a bang, leaving a smell of booze that would have tripped you up.

He takes a look at the quare fellow's side of the stage and, muttering to himself, goes back to work.

WARDER REGAN. You should pray for a man hardened in drink. Get back to it, all of you, and get that work a bit more advanced. Myself and Crimmin here have a long night ahead of us; we don't want to be finishing off your jobs for you.

They get into the grave.

PRISONER A. I never seen a screw like that before.

PRISONER B. Neither did anyone else.

They work.

CRIMMIN. What time is it, sir?

WARDER REGAN. Ten to seven.

CRIMMIN. Is himself here yet?

WARDER REGAN. Yes, he came by last night's boat. He's nervous of the 'plane, says it isn't natural. He'll be about soon. He's been having a sleep after the trip. We'll have to wait till he's measured the quare fellow for the drop, then we can go off till twelve.

CRIMMIN. Good.

WARDER REGAN. And for Christ's sake try to look a bit more cheerful when you come back on.

CRIMMIN. I've never seen anyone die, Mr. Regan.

WARDER REGAN. Of course, I'm a callous savage that's used to it.

CRIMMIN. I didn't mean that.

WARDER REGAN. I don't like it now any more than I did the first time.

CRIMMIN. No sir.

WARDER REGAN. It was a little Protestant lad, the first time; he asked if he could be walked backwards into the hanghouse so as he wouldn't see the rope.

CRIMMIN. God forgive them.

WARDER REGAN. May He forgive us all. The young clergyman that was on asked if the prison chaplain could accompany him; it was his first hanging too. I went to the Canon to ask him, a fine big man he was. "Regan," he says, "I thought I was going to escape it this time, but you never escape. I don't suppose neither of us ever will. Ah well," he says, "maybe being hung twenty times will get me out of purgatory a minute or two sooner."

CRIMMIN. Amen, a Thighearna Dhia.

WARDER REGAN. The young clergyman was great; he read a bit of the Bible to the little Protestant lad while they waited and he came in with him, holding his hand and telling him, in their way, to lean on God's mercy that was stronger than the power of men. I walked beside them and guided the boy on to the trap and under the beam. The rope was put round him and the washer under his ear and the hood pulled over his face. And still the young clergyman called out to him, in a grand steady voice, in through the hood: "I declare to you, my living Christ this night . . ." and he stroked his head till he went down. Then he fainted; the Canon and myself had to carry him out to the Governor's office.

A pause. We are aware of the men working at the grave.

WARDER REGAN. The quare fellow asked for you especially, Crimmin; he wanted you because you're a young lad, not yet practised in badness. You'll be a consolation to him in the morning when he's surrounded by a crowd of bigger bloody ruffians than himself, if the truth were but told. He's depending on you, and you're going to do your best for him.

CRIMMIN. Yes, Mr. Regan.

REGAN *walks to the grave.*

WARDER REGAN. How's it going?

PRISONER A. Just about done, sir.

WARDER REGAN. All right, you can leave it.

They get up.

WARDER REGAN. Leave your shovels; you'll be wanting them in the morning. Go and tell the warder they've finished, Mr. Crimmin. I'll turn them over.

He searches the PRISONERS, *finds a cigarette end on* A. *and sniffs it.*

Coffin nail. Most appropriate. [*He goes towards exit and calls.*] You needn't bother searching them, sir. I've turned them over.

PRISONER A. [*aside*]. He's as mad as a coot.

PRISONER C. But charitable.

WARDER REGAN. Right, lead on there!

PRISONER D. This is no place for charity, on the taxpayers' money.

PRISONER A. Take it up with your uncle when you get back into your stockbroker's trousers.

WARDER REGAN. Silence. Right, sir, working party off.

As the PRISONERS *march off, the* HANGMAN *comes slowly down the steps.*

CRIMMIN. Is this . . .

WARDER REGAN. Himself.

HANGMAN. It's Mr. Regan, isn't it? Well, as the girl said to the soldier "Here we are again."

WARDER REGAN. Nice evening. I hope you had a good crossing.

HANGMAN. Not bad. It's nice to get over to old Ireland you know, a nice bit of steak and a couple of pints as soon as you get off the boat. Well, you'll be wanting to knock off, won't you? I'll just pop down and have a look, then you can knock off.

WARDER REGAN. We were just waiting for you.

HANGMAN. This young man coming with us in the morning?

CRIMMIN. Yes, sir.

HANGMAN. Lend us your cap a minute, lad.

CRIMMIN. I don't think it would fit you, sir.

HANGMAN. We don't have to be so particular. Mr. Regan's will do. It ought to fit me by this time, and he won't catch cold the time I'll be away.

He goes out.

CRIMMIN. What does he want the cap for?

WARDER REGAN. He gets the quare fellow's weight from the doctor so as he'll know what drop to give him, but he likes to have a look at him as well, to see what build he is, how thick his neck is, and so on. He says he can judge better with the eye. If he gave him too much one way he'd strangle him instead of breaking his neck, and too much the other way he'd pull the head clean off his shoulders.

CRIMMIN. Go bhoiridh Dia orainm.

WARDER REGAN. You should have lent him your cap. When he lifts the corner of the spy-hole all the quare fellow can see is the peak of a warder's cap. It could be you or me or anyone looking at him. Himself has no more to do with it than you or I or the people that pay us, and that's every man or woman that pays taxes or votes in elections. If they don't like it, they needn't have it.

The HANGMAN *comes back.*

HANGMAN. Well set up lad. Twelve stone, fine pair of shoulders on him. Well, I expect you'll give us a call this evening over at the hospital. I'm in my usual apartments. This young man is very welcome, too, if he wants to join the company.

WARDER REGAN. Right, sir.

HANGMAN. See you later.

He goes out.

WARDER REGAN. Right, Crimmin. Twelve o'clock and look lively. The quare fellow's got enough on his plate without putting him in the blue jigs altogether. As the old Home Office memorandum says "An air of cheerful decorum is indicated, as a readiness to play such games as draughts, ludo, or snakes and ladders; a readiness to enter into conversations on sporting topics will also be appreciated."

CRIMMIN. Yes, sir.

WARDER REGAN. [*as they go*]. And, Crimmin, . . .

CRIMMIN. Yes, sir?

WARDER REGAN. Take off your watch.

They go out.

NEIGHBOUR [*from his cell*]. Hey, Dunlavin. Don't forget that Sunday bacon. The bet stands. They're after being at the grave. I just heard them. Dunlavin, do you hear me?

PRISONER A. Get down on your bed, you old Anti-Christ. You sound like something in a week-end pass out of Hell.

ENGLISH PRISONER. Hey, you bloke that's going out in the morning. Don't forget to see my chiner and get him to bail me out.

NEIGHBOUR. Get a bucket and bail yourself out.

SONG. The day was dying and the wind was sighing,
As I lay crying in my prison cell,
And the old triangle
Went jingle jangle
Along the banks of the Royal Canal.

The curtain falls

ACT III

Scene One

Later the same night. Cell windows lit. A blue lamp in the courtyard. A faint tapping is heard intermittently.

As the curtain rises, two WARDERS *are seen. One is* DONELLY, *the other a fellow new to the job.*

WARDER 1. Watch the match.

WARDER 2. Sorry.

WARDER 1. We're all right for a couple of minutes, the Chief'll have plenty to worry him tonight; he's not likely to be prowling about.

WARDER 2. Hell of a job, night patrol, at any time.

WARDER 1. We're supposed to pass each cell every half-hour tonight, but what's the use? Listen to 'em.

The tapping can be distinctly heard.

WARDER 2. Yap, yap, yap. It's a wonder the bloody old hot-water pipes aren't worn through.

Tapping.

WARDER 1. Damn it all, they've been yapping in association since seven o'clock.

Tapping.

WARDER 2. Will I go round the landings and see who it is?

WARDER 1. See who it is? Listen!

WARDER 2. Do you think I should go?

WARDER 1. Stay where you are and get yourself a bit of a burn. Devil a bit of use it'd be anyway. As soon as you lifted the first spy-hole, the next fellow would have heard you and passed it on to the whole landing. Mind the cigarette, keep it covered. Have you ever been in one of these before?

WARDER 2. No.

WARDER 1. They'll be at it from six o'clock tomorrow morning, and when it comes a quarter to eight it'll be like a running commentary in the Grand National.

Tapping.

WARDER 1 [*quietly*]. Shut your bloody row! And then the screeches and roars of them when his time comes. They say it's the last thing the fellow hears.

Tapping dies down.

WARDER 2. Talk about something else.

Tapping.

WARDER 1. They're quietening down a bit. You'd think they'd be in the humour for a read or a sleep, wouldn't you?

WARDER 2. It's a hell of a job.

WARDER 1. We're in it for the three P's, boy, pay, promotion and pension, that's all that should bother civil servants like us.

WARDER 2. You're quite right.

WARDER 1. And without doing the sergeant major on you, I'm senior man of us two, isn't that right, now?

WARDER 2. I know what you mean.

WARDER 1. Well, neither bragging nor boasting—God gives

us the brains and no credit to ourselves—I think I might speak to you as a senior man, if you didn't mind.

WARDER 2. Not at all. Any tip you could give me I'd be only too grateful for it. Sure it'd only be a thick wouldn't improve his knowledge when an older man would be willing to tell him something that would be of benefit to him in his career.

WARDER 1. Well now, would I be right in saying that you've no landing of your own?

WARDER 2. Quite right, quite right. I'm only on here, there or any old where when you or any other senior man is wanting me.

WARDER 1. Well, facts is facts and must be faced. We must all creep before we can walk, as the man said; but I may as well tell you straight, what I told the Principal about you.

WARDER 2. Tell me face to face. If it's fault you found in me I'd as lief hear it from me friend as from me enemy.

WARDER 1. It was no fault I found in you. If I couldn't do a man a good turn—I'd be sorry to do him a bad one.

WARDER 2. Ah, sure I know that.

WARDER 1. What I said to the Principal about you was: that you could easily handle a landing of your own. If it happened that one was left vacant. And I don't think I'm giving official information away, when I say that such a vacancy may occur in the near future. Before the month is out. Have you me?

WARDER 2. I have you, and I'm more than grateful to you. But sure I'd expect no less from you. You're all nature.

WARDER 1. It might happen that our Principal was going to the Bog on promotion, and it might happen that a certain senior officer would be promoted in his place.

WARDER 2. Ah, no.

WARDER 1. But ah, yes.

WARDER 2. But there's no one in the prison but'd be delighted to serve under you. You've such a way with you. Even with the prisoners.

WARDER 1. Well, I hope I can do my best by me fellow men, and that's the most any can hope to do, barring a double-dyed bloody hypocrite like a certain party we needn't mention. Well, him and me have equal service and it's only the one of us can be made Principal, and I'm damn sure they're not going to appoint a half-lunatic that goes round asking murderers to pray for him.

WARDER 2. Certainly they're not, unless they're bloody-well half-mad themselves.

WARDER 1. And I think they know him as well as we do.

WARDER 2. Except the Canon, poor man; he has him well recommended.

WARDER 1. You can leave out the "poor man" part of it. God forgive me and I renounce the sin of it, the Lord says "touch not my anointed", but the Canon is a bloody sight worse than himself, if you knew only the half of it.

WARDER 2. Go to God.

WARDER 1. Right, I'll tell you now. He was silenced for something before he came here and this is the *only* job he can get. Something terrible he did, though God forgive us, maybe it's not right to talk of it.

WARDER 2. You might sing it.

WARDER 1. I hear it was the way that he made the housekeeper take a girl into the house, the priest's house, to have a baby, an illegitimate!

WARDER 2. And could a man like that be fit to be a priest!

WARDER 1. He'd hardly be fit to be a prison chaplain, even. Here's the Chief or one of them coming. Get inside quick and let on you're looking for them fellows talking on the hot-water pipes, and not a word about what I said. That's between ourselves.

WARDER 2. Ah sure I know that's under foot. Thanks anyway.

WARDER 1. You're more than welcome. Don't be surprised if you get your landing sooner than you expected. Thirty cells all to yourself before you're fifty.

WARDER 2. I'll have the sister's children pray for you.

Enter CHIEF WARDER.

WARDER 1. All correct, sir.

CHIEF. What the hell do you mean, "All correct, sir"? I've been watching you this half-hour yapping away to that other fellow.

WARDER 1. There were men communicating on the hot-water pipes, sir, and I told him ten times if I told him once to go inside the landing and see who it was; it's my opinion, sir, the man is a bit thick.

CHIEF. It's your opinion. Well, you're that thick yourself you ought to be a fair judge. And who the bloody hell are you to tell anyone to do anything? You're on night patrol the same as what he is.

WARDER 1. I thought, sir, on account of the night that's in it.

CHIEF. Why, is it Christmas? Listen here, that there is an execution in the morning is nothing to do with you. It's not your job to care, and a good job too, or you'd probably trip over the rope and fall through the bloody trap. What business have you out here, anyway?

WARDER 1. I thought I had to patrol by the grave, sir.

CHIEF. Afraid somebody might pinch it? True enough, this place is that full of thieves, you can leave nothing out of your hand. Get inside and resume your patrol. If you weren't one of the old hands I'd report you to the Governor. Get along with you and we'll forget about it.

WARDER 1. Very good, sir, and thank you, sir.

Tapping.

CHIEF. And stop that tapping on the pipes.

WARDER 1. I will, sir, and thanks again, sir.

FIRST WARDER *salutes, goes up the steps to the prison gates, which open. The* GOVERNOR *comes in in evening dress. The* FIRST WARDER *comes sharply to attention, salutes and goes off. The* GOVERNOR *continues down the steps and over to the* CHIEF WARDER.

CHIEF. All correct, sir.

GOVERNOR. Good. We had final word about the reprieve this afternoon. But you know how these things are, Chief, hoping for last-minute developments. I must say I should have been more than surprised had the Minister made a recommendation. I'll go down and see him before the Canon comes in. It makes them more settled for confession when they know there is absolutely no hope. How is he?

CHIEF. Very well, sir. Sitting by the fire and chatting to the warders. He says he might go to bed after he sees the priest.

GOVERNOR. You'll see that there's a good breakfast for himself and the two assistants?

CHIEF. Oh, yes, sir, he's very particular about having two rashers and eggs. Last time they were here, some hungry pig ate half his breakfast and he kicked up murder.

GOVERNOR. See it doesn't happen this time.

CHIEF. No indeed. There's a fellow under sentence of death next week in the Crumlin; we don't want him going up to Belfast and saying we starved him.

GOVERNOR. Have they come back from town yet?

CHIEF [*looks at his watch*]. It's after closing time. I don't expect they'll be long now. I put Clancy on the side gate to let them in. After he took the quare fellow's measurements he went over to the place he drinks in. Some pub at the top of Grafton Street. I believe he's the life of the bar there, sir; the customers think he's an English traveller. The publican knows who he is, but then they're both in the pub business, and sure that's as tight a trade as hanging.

GOVERNOR. I suppose his work here makes him philosophical, and they say that drink is the comfort of the philosophers.

CHIEF. I wouldn't doubt but you'd be right there, sir. But he told me himself he only takes a drink when he's on a job. The rest of the time he's serving behind his own bar.

GOVERNOR. Is Jenkinson with him?

CHIEF. Yes, sir. He likes to have him with him, in case he gets a bit jarred. Once he went straight from the boat to the pubs and spent the day in them, and when he got here wasn't he after leaving the black box with his rope and his washers and his other little odds and ends behind him in a pub and forgot which one it was he left them in.

GOVERNOR. Really.

CHIEF. You could sing it. You were in Limerick at the time, sir, but here we were, in a desperate state. An execution coming off in the morning and we without the black box that had all his tools in it. The Governor we had then, he promised a novena to St. Anthony and two insertions in the *Messenger* if they were found in time. And sure enough after squad cars were all over in the city, the box was got in a pub down the North Wall, the first one he went into. It shows you the power of prayer, sir.

GOVERNOR. Yes, I see what you mean.

CHIEF. So now he always brings Jenkinson with him. You see, Jenkinson takes nothing, being very good living. A street preacher he is, for the Methodists or something. Himself prefers T.T.s. He had an Irishman from Clare helping one time, but he sacked him over the drink. In this Circus, he said, there's only one allowed to drink and that's the Ringmaster.

GOVERNOR. We advertised for a native hangman during the Economic War. Must be fluent Irish speaker. Cauliochtai do rior Meamram V.7. There were no suitable applicants.

CHIEF. By the way, sir, I must tell you that the warders on night patrol were out here conversing, instead of going round the landings.

GOVERNOR. Remind me to make a note of it tomorrow.

CHIEF. I will, sir, and I think I ought to tell you that I heard the principal warder make a joke about the execution.

GOVERNOR. Good God, this sort of thing is getting out of hand. I was at my School Union this evening. I had to leave in sheer embarrassment; supposedly witty remarks made to me at my own table. My eldest son was furious with me for going at all. He was at a table with a crowd from the University. They were even worse. One young pup went so far as to ask him if he thought I would oblige with a rendering of "The night before Larry was stretched". I shall certainly tell the Principal that there's at least one place in this city where an execution is taken very seriously indeed. Good night to you.

CHIEF. Good night, sir.

Tapping. The CHIEF WARDER *walks up and down.* REGAN *enters.*

Ah, Mr. Regan, the other man coming along?

WARDER REGAN. He'll be along in a minute.

CHIEF. I don't know what we'd do without you, Regan, on these jobs. Is there anything the Governor or I could do to make things easier?

WARDER REGAN. You could say a decade of the rosary.

CHIEF. I could hardly ask the Governor to do that.

WARDER REGAN. His prayers would be as good as anyone else's.

CHIEF. Is there anything on the practical side we could send down?

WARDER REGAN. A bottle of malt.

CHIEF. Do you think he'd drink it?

WARDER REGAN. No, but I would.

CHIEF. Regan, I'm surprised at you.

WARDER REGAN. I was reared among people that drank at a death or prayed. Some did both. You think the law makes this man's death someway different, not like anyone else's. Your own, for instance.

CHIEF. I wasn't found guilty of murder.

WARDER REGAN. No, nor no one is going to jump on you in the morning and throttle the life out of you, but it's not him I'm thinking of. It's myself. And you're not going to give me that stuff about just shoving over the lever and bob's your uncle. You forget the times the fellow gets caught and has to be kicked off the edge of the trap hole. You never heard of the warders down below swinging on his legs the better to break his neck, or jumping on his back when the drop was too short.

CHIEF. Mr. Regan, I'm surprised at you.

WARDER REGAN. That's the second time tonight.

Tapping. Enter CRIMMIN.

CRIMMIN. All correct, sir.

CHIEF. Regan, I hope you'll forget those things you mentioned just now. If talk the like of that got outside the prison . . .

WARDER REGAN [*almost shouts*]. I think the whole show should be put on in Croke Park; after all, it's at the public expense and they let it go on. They should have something more for their money than a bit of paper stuck up on the gate.

CHIEF. Good night, Regan. If I didn't know you, I'd report what you said to the Governor.

WARDER REGAN. You will anyway.

CHIEF. Good night, Regan.

WARDER REGAN [*to* CRIMMIN]. Crimmin, there you are. I'm going into the hospital to fix up some supper for us. An empty sack won't stand, as the man said, nor a full one won't bend.

He goes. CRIMMIN *strolls. Traffic is heard in the distance. drowning the tapping. A drunken crowd are heard singing.* DONELLY *and the* NEW WARDER *appear in the darkness.*

WARDER 1. Is that young Mr. Crimmin?

CRIMMIN. Yes, it's me.

WARDER 1. You've a desperate job for a young warder this night. But I'll tell you one thing, you've a great man with you. Myself and this other man here are only after being talking about him.

WARDER 2. That's right, so we were. A grand man and very good living.

WARDER 1. There's someone coming. Too fine a night to be indoors. Good night, Mr. Crimmin.

CRIMMIN. Good night, sir.

WARDER 1 [*as they go off*]. Come on, let's get a sup of tea.

CRIMMIN *waits. Tapping heard.* WARDER REGAN *re-enters.*

WARDER REGAN. Supper's fixed. It's a fine clear night. Do you hear the buses? Fellows leaving their mot's home, after the pictures or coming from dances, and a few old fellows well jarred but half sober for fear of what herself will say when they get in the door. Only a hundred yards up there on the bridge, and it might as well be a hundred miles away. Here they are back from the pub.

Voices are heard in the dark approaching. Enter HANGMAN *and* JENKINSON.

HANGMAN [*sings*].

"She was lovely and fair like the rose of the summer,
Though 'twas not her beauty alone that won me,
Oh, no, 'twas the truth in her eyes ever shining,
That made me love Mary the Rose of Tralee."

Don't see any signs of Regan.

JENKINSON. He's probably had to go on duty. You've left it too late.

HANGMAN. Well, if the mountain won't come to M'ammed then the M'ammed must go to the mountain.

WARDER REGAN [*from the darkness*]. As the girl said to the soldier.

HANGMAN. As the girl said to the soldier. Oh, it's you, Regan. Will you have a drink?

WARDER REGAN. I'm afraid we've got to be off now.

HANGMAN. Never mind off now. Have one with me. It's a pleasure to see you again. We meet all too seldom. You have one with me. Adam, give him a bottle of stout.

He sings again.

"Oh, no, 'twas the truth in her eyes ever shining,
That made me love Mary the Rose of Tralee."

Not bad for an old 'un. Lovely song, in't it? Very religious though. "The Poor Christian Fountain." I'm very fond of the old Irish songs; we get a lot of Irish in our place on a Saturday night, you know.

WARDER REGAN. Is it what they call a sporting pub?

HANGMAN. That's just what it is, and an old sport behind the bar counter an' all. All the Irish come in, don't they, Adam?

JENKINSON [*gloomily*]. Reckon they do. Perhaps because no one else would go in it.

HANGMAN. What do you mean? It's best beer in the district. Not that you could tell the difference.

WARDER REGAN. Good health.

HANGMAN. May we never do worse. [*To* JENKINSON.] You're in a right cut, aren't you, making out there's nobody but Irish coming into my pub? I've never wanted for friends. Do you know why? Because I'd go a 'undred mile to do a man a good turn. I've always tried to do my duty.

JENKINSON. And so have I.

HANGMAN. Do you remember the time I got out from a sickbed to 'ang a soldier at Strangeways, when I thought you and Christmas 'adn't had enough experience?

JENKINSON. Aye, that's right enough.

HANGMAN. I'm not going to quarrel with you. Here, go and fetch your concertina and sing 'em that hymn you composed.

JENKINSON *hesitates.*

HANGMAN. Go on. It's a grand tune, a real credit to you. Go on, lad.

JENKINSON. Well, only for the hymn, mind.

He goes off to fetch it.

WARDER REGAN. Sure, that's right.

HANGMAN. 'E's a good lad is our Adam, but 'e's down in the dumps at the moment. 'Im and Christmas, they used to sing on street corners with the Band of Holy Joy, every Saturday night, concertina and all. But some of the lads found out who they were and started putting bits of rope in collection boxes; it's put them off outdoor testimony. But this 'ymn's very moving about hanging and mercy and so forth. Brings tears to your eyes to 'ear Adam and Christmas singing it.

JENKINSON *returns.*

JENKINSON. Right?

HANGMAN. Right!

JENKINSON [*sings*].

My brother, sit and think.
While yet some time is left to thee
Kneel to thy God who from thee does not shrink
And lay thy sins on Him who died for thee.

HANGMAN. Take a fourteen-stone man as a basis and giving him a drop of eight foot . . .

JENKINSON.

Men shrink from thee but not I,
Come close to me I love my erring sheep.
My blood can cleanse thy sins of blackest dye,
I understand if thou canst only weep.

HANGMAN. Every half-stone lighter would require a two-inch longer drop, so for weight thirteen and a half stone—drop eight feet two inches, and for weight thirteen stone—drop eight feet four inches.

JENKINSON.

Though thou hast grieved me sore,
My arms of mercy still are open wide,
I still hold open Heaven's shining door
Come then, take refuge in my wounded side.

HANGMAN. Now he's only twelve stone so he should have eight foot eight, but he's got a thick neck on him so I'd better give him another couple of inches. Yes, eight foot ten.

JENKINSON.

Come now, the time is short.
Longing to pardon and bless I wait.
Look up to me, my sheep so dearly bought
And say, forgive me, ere it is too late.

HANGMAN. Divide 412 by the weight of the body in stones, multiply by two gives the length of the drop in inches. [*He looks up and seems sobered.*] 'E's an R.C., I suppose, Mr. Regan? [*Puts book in his pocket.*]

WARDER REGAN. That's right.

HANGMAN. That's all, then. Good night.

JENKINSON. Good night.

WARDER REGAN. Good night. [*The* HANGMAN *and* JENKINSON *go off.*] Thanks for the hymn. Great night for stars. If there's life on any of them, I wonder do the same things happen up there? Maybe some warders on a planet are walking across a prison yard this minute and some fellow up there waiting on the rope in the morning, and looking out through the bars, for a last look at our earth and the moon for the last time. Though I never saw them to bother much about things like that. It's nearly always letters to their wives or mothers, and then we don't send them—only throw them into the grave after them. What'd be the sense of broadcasting such distressful rubbish?

PRISONER C. [*sings from his cell window*]. Is e fath mo bhuadhartha na bhaghaim cead curts.

WARDER REGAN. Regular choir practice going on round here tonight.

CRIMMIN. He's singing for . . . for . . .

WARDER REGAN. For the quare fellow.

CRIMMIN. Yes. Why did the Englishman ask if he was a Catholic?

WARDER REGAN. So as they'd know to have the hood slit to anoint him on the rope, and so as the fellows below would know to take off his boots and socks for the holy oil on his feet when he goes down.

PRISONER C. [*sings*]. N'il gaoth adtuaidh ann,
N'il sneachta cruaidh ann . . .

WARDER REGAN. We'd better be getting in. The other screws will be hopping mad to get out; they've been there since four o'clock today.

PRISONER C. [*sings*]. Mo whuirnin bhan . . .

His song dies away and the empty stage is gradually lightened for

Scene Two

The prison yard. It is morning.

WARDER 1. How's the time?

WARDER 2. Seven minutes.

WARDER 1. As soon as it goes five to eight they'll start. You'd think they were working with stop watches. I wish I was at home having my breakfast. How's the time?

WARDER 2. Just past six minutes.

MICKSER'S VOICE. Bail o dhis orribh go leir a chairdre.

WARDER 1. I knew it. That's that bloody Mickser. I'll fix him this time.

MICKSER'S VOICE. And we take you to the bottom of D. Wing.

WARDER 1. You bastard, I'll give you D. Wing.

MICKSER'S VOICE. We're ready for the start, and in good time, and who do I see lined up for the off but the High Sheriff of this ancient city of ours, famous in song and story as the place where the pig ate the whitewash brushes and—[*The* WARDERS *remove their caps.*] We're off, in this order: the Governor, the Chief, two screws Regan and Crimmin, the quare fellow between them, two more screws and three runners from across the Channel, getting well in front, now the Canon. He's making a big effort for the last two furlongs. He's got the white pudding bag on his head, just a short distance to go. He's in.

[*A clock begins to chime the hour. Each quarter sounds louder.*] His feet to the chalk line. He'll be pinioned, his feet together. The bag will be pulled down over his face. The screws come off the trap and steady him. Himself goes to the lever and . . .

The hour strikes. The WARDERS *cross themselves and put on their caps. From the* PRISONERS *comes a ferocious howling.*

PRISONERS. One off, one away, one off, one away.

WARDER 1. Shut up there.

WARDER 2. Shut up, shut up.

WARDER 1. I know your windows, I'll get you. Shut up.

The noise dies down and at last ceases altogether.

Now we'll go in and get that Mickser. [*Grimly.*] *I'll* soften his cough. Come on . . .

WARDER REGAN *comes out.*

WARDER REGAN. Give us a hand with this fellow.

WARDER 1. We're going after that Mickser.

WARDER REGAN. Never mind that now, give us a hand. He fainted when the trap was sprung.

WARDER 1. These young screws, not worth a light.

They carry CRIMMIN *across the yard.*

NEIGHBOUR'S VOICE. Dunlavin, that's a Sunday bacon you owe me. Your man was topped, wasn't he?

PRISONER A.'S VOICE. You won't be long after him.

DUNLAVIN'S VOICE. Don't mind him, Neighbour.

NEIGHBOUR'S VOICE. Don't you forget that bacon, Dunlavin.

DUNLAVIN'S VOICE. I forgot to tell you, Neighbour.

NEIGHBOUR'S VOICE. What did you forget to tell me?

ENGLISH VOICE. Where's the bloke what's going out this morning?

NEIGHBOUR'S VOICE. He's up in Nelly's room behind the clock. What about that bacon, Dunlavin?

ENGLISH VOICE. You bloke that's going out this morning, remember to see my chiner and tell him to 'ave me bailed out.

NEIGHBOUR'S VOICE. Get a bucket and bail yourself out. What about me bacon, Dunlavin?

ENGLISH VOICE. Sod you and your bleeding bacon.

DUNLAVIN'S VOICE. Shut up a minute about your bail, till I tell Neighbour about his bet.

NEIGHBOUR'S VOICE. You lost it, that's all I know.

DUNLAVIN'S VOICE. Yes, but the doctor told me that me stomach was out of order; he's put me on a milk diet.

CHIEF [*comes through prison gates and looks up*]. Get down from those windows. Get down at once. [*He beckons inside and* PRISONERS A., B., C. *and* D. *file past him and go down on the steps.* PRISONER B. *is carrying a cold hammer and chisel.*] Hey, you there in front, have you the cold chisel and hammer?

PRISONER B. Yes, sir.

CHIEF. You other three, the shovels are where you left them; get to work there and clear the top and have it ready for filling in.

They go on to the canvas, take up the shovels from behind and begin work. PRISONER B. *stands on the foot of the steps with his cold chisel while the* CHIEF *studies his paper to give final instructions.*

CHIEF. Yes, that's it. You're to carve E.777. Got that?

PRISONER B. Yes, sir. E.777.

CHIEF. That's it. It should be E.779 according to the book, but a "7" is easier for you to do than a "9". Right, the stone in the wall that's nearest to the spot. Go ahead now. [*Raising his voice.*] There's the usual two bottles of stout a man, but only if you work fast.

WARDER 1. I know the worst fellow was making this noise, sir. It was Mickser, sir. I'm going in to case him now. I'll take an hour's overtime to do it, sir.

CHIEF. You're a bit late. He was going out this morning and had his civilian clothing on in the cell. We were only waiting for this to be over to let him out.

WARDER 1. But . . . Sir, he was the whole cause.

CHIEF. Well, what do you want me to do, run down the Circular Road after him? He went out on remission. We could have stopped him. But you were too bloody slow for that.

WARDER 1. I was helping to carry . . .

CHIEF. You were helping to carry . . . Warders! I'd get better in Woolworths.

WARDER 2. To think of that dirty savage getting away like that. Shouting and a man going to his God.

WARDER 1. Never mind that part of it. He gave me lip in the woodyard in '42, and I couldn't do anything because he was only on remand. I've been waiting years to get that fellow.

WARDER 2. Ah, well, you've one consolation. He'll be back.

At the grave PRISONER A. *is the only one visible over the canvas.*

PRISONER B. Would you say that this was the stone in the wall nearest to it?

PRISONER A. It'll do well enough. It's only for the records. They're not likely to be digging him up to canonize him.

PRISONER B. Fair enough. E.777.

REGAN *drops the letters into the grave, and goes.*

PRISONER A. Give us them bloody letters. They're worth money to one of the Sunday papers.

PRISONER B. So I understood you to say yesterday.

PRISONER A. Well, give us them.

PRISONER D. They're not exclusively your property any more than anyone else's.

PRISONER B. There's no need to have a battle over them. Divide them. Anyone that likes can have my share and I suppose the same goes for the kid.

PRISONER D. Yes, we can act like businessmen. There are three. One each and toss for the third. I'm a businessman.

PRISONER A. Fair enough. Amn't I a businessman myself? For what's a crook, only a businessman without a shop.

PRISONER D. What side are you on? The blank side or the side with the address?

VOICE OF PRISONER BELOW [*singing*].

In the female prison
There are seventy women
I wish it was with them that I did dwell,
Then that old triangle
Could jingle jangle
Along the banks of the Royal Canal.

The curtain falls.

The Hostage

"The Hostage" was first presented by Theatre Workshop at the Theatre Royal, Stratford, London, E.15, on 14th October, 1958, with the following cast:

PAT, *the caretaker of a lodging-house*	Howard Goorney
MEG DILLON	Avis Bunnage
MONSEWER, *the owner of the house*	Glynn Edwards
COLETTE	Leila Greenwood
BOBO	Annette Robertson
PRINCESS GRACE	Dudley Sutton
RIO RITA	Roy Barnett
MR. MULLEADY	Robin Chapman
MISS GILCHRIST, *a social worker*	Eileen Kennally
LESLIE, *a British soldier*	Murray Melvin
TERESA, *a country girl*	Celia Salkeld
I.R.A. OFFICER	James Booth
VOLUNTEER	Clive Barker

SAILORS, WHORES, POLICEMEN, ETC.

The play produced by Joan Littlewood

ACT I

Curtain up.

Whole company dances an Irish Jig after two figures in which two whores and two queers have danced together; MULLEADY *is seen dancing with* MISS GILCHRIST.

1ST WHORE [*to* QUEERS]. Get off the stage, you dirty low things.

COLETTE. A decent whore can't get a shilling round here for the likes of you.

PRINCESS GRACE. To hell with you, and your friends in America. Come on, dear [*to* RIO], take no notice of them.

1ST WHORE. Go, get a mass said for yourself.

PRINCESS GRACE. What we need round here is a bit of tolerance.

Exit whores and queers.

A blast on bagpipes.

MEG. In the name of God, what's that?

PAT. It's only Monsewer practising his music. He has taken it into his head to play the Dead March for the boy in Belfast Jail when they hang him in the morning.

MEG. I wish he'd keep it in his head. Those bagpipes get on my nerves.

PAT. Get us a bottle of stout.

MEG. Get it yourself.

PAT. I'm not able.

MEG. Of course you're able.

PAT. Begod, the old leg's killing me tonight. I've a cruel pain where it used to be.

MEG. Get along with you, you old scow. Do you think they will hang him.

PAT. Who?

MEG. The boy in Belfast Jail.

PAT. There's no think about it. Tomorrow morning at the hour of eight, he'll hang as high as Killymanjaaro.

MEG. What the hell's that?

PAT. It's a noted mountain off the south coast of Switzerland. It would do you the world of no good to be hung as high as it, anyway.

MEG. Do you know what he said? "As a soldier of the Irish Republic, I will die smiling."

PAT. And who asked him to give himself the trouble?

MEG. He only did his duty as a member of the I.R.A.

PAT. Don't have me to use a coarse expression, you silly old bitch. This is nineteen-fifty-eight, and the days of the heroes is over this thirty-five years past. Long over, finished and done with. The I.R.A. and the War of Independence are as dead—as dead as the Charleston.

MEG. The old cause is never dead, till Ireland will be free from the centre to the sea. Hurrah for liberty, says the Shan Van Vocht.

PAT [*sighs*]. She's as bad as Monsewer. It's bad enough for that old idiot not to have a clock, but I declare to Jesus, I don't think he even has a calendar. And who has all the trouble of it? I have. He wants to have the new I.R.A., so called, in this place now. "Prepare a room for them," no less. Bad enough running this place as a speak-easy and a brockel—

MEG. A what?

PAT. A brockel—that's English for a whorehouse.

MEG. I will be thankful to you to keep that kind of talk about whorehouses to yourself. I'm no whore for one!

PAT. Why? Are you after losing your union card?

MEG. Well, if I'm a whore itself, you don't mind taking the best part of my money. So you're nothing but a ponce.

PAT. Well, I'm saving up to be one! [*Mutters.*] And a good while that'll take with the money you earn.

MEG. Oh it will.

PAT. Yes.

MEG. Well, you know what you can do.

They sit with their backs to each other.

PAT. You ought to know better than to abuse me, a poor crippled man that lost his leg on the field of slaughter, three miles outside the town of Mullingar. And how do you think any of us could keep the house going on what I get from Monsewer? And who would look after him, in England or Ireland, if I didn't? I stick by him, because we were soldiers of Ireland in the old days: can I sing my old song to him?

MEG. I suppose so.

PAT [*sings*]:

On the eighteenth day of November,
Just outside the town of Macroom,
The 'Tans in their big Crossley tenders,
Came roaring along to their doom,
But the boys of the column were waiting
With hand grenades primed on the spot,
And the Irish Republican Army
Made quit of the whole bleeding lot.

MEG. You're always singing about them ould times, and the five glorious years, and still you sneer and jeer at the boys nowadays. What's the difference?

PAT. The H-Bomb. I'm nervous of it. It's such a big bomb it's after making me scared of little bombs. The I.R.A. is out of date and so is the R.A.F. So is the Swiss Guard and the Foreign Legion, the Red Army, the United States Marines, the Free State Army.

MEG. And the Civic Guards?

PAT. The Coldstream Guards, the Scots Guards, the Welsh Guards, the Grenadier Guards—

The sound of the pipes again. This time they are playing "O'Donnell Aboo".

MEG. Here is Monsewer, now.

PAT [*puts his two hands over his ears*]. I hear him. Jasus, amn't I deaf with him?

Enter MONSEWER. *He is a tall man, with a large white moustache. He is wearing a kilt, and carries his pipes with a noble air. He blows a last long note on the pipes.*

MONSEWER. Good day to you.

PAT [*coming to attention like an old soldier*]. Commandant-General!

MONSEWER [*salutes*]. As you were. [*He nods towards* MEG.)

PAT [*to* MEG]. Go out there and be sweeping the stairs.

[MEG *takes the hint and goes out.*]

Well, the room is cleaned out and prepared as you see.

MONSEWER. Good, good. The troops will be coming quite soon.

PAT [*aside*]. The troops. Good God. [*To* MONSEWER.] How many of them are expected, then.

MONSEWER. There will be the two guards and the prisoner.

PAT. The prisoner?

MONSEWER. Yes. Yes, we only have the one at the moment, but it's a good beginning.

PAT. Yes, indeed, as the Scotchman says, "Many a mickle makes a muckle."

MONSEWER. And as we Irish say, "It was one after another they built the castles—Iss in yeeg a kale-ah shah togeock nuh cashlawn."

PAT. That's Irish. Isn't it great for them that has an Oxford University education. God help me, I'm only a poor ignorant Dublin man. I wouldn't understand a word of it. The prisoner you were talking about, sir?

MONSEWER. Yes. An English soldier they captured in Armagh last night. One only. But that's only the beginning. Before long we'll have scores of them.

PAT [*aside*]. I hope to God he's not going to bring them all here.

MONSEWER. What's that?

PAT [*in a louder tone*]. It's a great thing, I say, that the boys are out again.

MONSEWER. It's wonderful. Carry on. [*Exit.*]

MEG. He's a decent old skin, even if he has got a slate loose.

PAT. Did you hear that? I thought it was bad enough making a sort of I.R.A. barracks out of this place, but it's worse than that. Monsewer is going to make a glasshouse out of it. A kind of private Shepton Mallet of his own.

MEG. We should be proud to help the men that are fighting for Ireland. Especially that poor boy to be hanged in Belfast Jail tomorrow morning.

PAT. Why are you getting so upset over Ireland? Where the hell were you in nineteen-sixteen when the real fighting was going on?

MEG. I wasn't born.

PAT [*throws up his two hands*]. You're full of excuses! Where the hell were they when we had to go out and capture our own stuff off of the British Army?

MEG. You told me that you bought it off the Tommies in the pub. You said yourself you got a revolver, two hundred rounds of ammunition, and a pair of jodhpurs off a colonel's batman for two pints of Bass and fifty Woodbines.

PAT. I shouldn't have given him anything. But I was sorry for him.

MEG. Why?

PAT. He was engaged to my sister-in-law.

There is a sound of a row upstairs. MR. MULLEADY *rushes down.*

MR. MULLEADY. Oh! Mr. Pat, something terrible is happening!

PAT. What's going on?

COLETTE [*yelling*]. Get out, you dirty foreign bastard.

SAILOR *protests in Polish.*

Do you know what he is? A Pole, he is. Off one of the Polish coal boats that's just in. Pat, will you give us a hand? Mr. Mulleady told me just now, he's a Pole, he is.

PAT. What's wrong with that? Is he dirty or something?

MR. MULLEADY. Worse than that, Mr. Pat. He's a communist, that's what's wrong with it, my friend. [MEG *moves away from him.*]

COLETTE. Go on out.

PAT. What's got into you?

MEG. Pat, it's against my religion, I tell you, to have to do with the likes of him.

MR. MULLEADY. That's what I told her.

PAT. Ah, sure you have to pick up trade where you can get it these days.

MR. MULLEADY. Mr. Pat, I'm surprised at you saying a thing like that.

COLETTE. Will you throw him out of here?

PAT. The only reason I know for throwing a man out is when he has no money to pay.

MEG. Has he got any?

POLE. Da?

PAT. I'll find out. Got any gelt? Dollars? Pound notes? Money?

POLE. Oh da, da.

Empties pockets, which have many notes in them. Offers them to COLETTE.

MEG. Do you see the wad he has on him?

COLETTE *crosses herself then takes some.* MR. MULLEADY *picks one up.*

COLETTE. Come on.

MEG. Pound notes is the best religion in the world.

PAT. And the best politics.

MONSEWER *enters—he speaks in Irish to the* POLE, *who responds in* POLISH.

MONSEWER. Carry on, my dear. Ireland needs the work of women as well, you know. [*Exit.*]

COLETTE. I know that, Monsewer. And a bed in heaven to you.

PAT *indicates that the* POLE *should go up with* COLETTE.

POLE. Spasiba. [*Exeunt* POLE *and* COLETTE.]

PAT. And the same to you.

MR. MULLEADY. I'm sorry Mrs. M.—I mean about the Pole. I felt that as a God-fearing man I could shut my eyes no longer.

PAT. It's a pity you don't close them indefinitely.

MEG. Ah, get along with you. Anybody would think you was doing God a good turn speaking well of him.

MR. MULLEADY. Oh, and another thing—about my laundry, Miss Meg. It was due back three days ago. I have to go to one of my committees this evening and I haven't a shirt to my name.

PAT. It walked back.

MEG. Go and ask the Prisoners Aid Society to help you.

MR. MULLEADY. You know very well that that is the committee on which I serve.

MEG. Well, go and wash one.

MR. MULLEADY. You know I can't . . .

MEG. Get going, or I'll ask you for the money you owe me.

MR. MULLEADY. Please don't bring all that up again. You know that at the end of the month . . .

MEG. Are you going . . . [MR. MULLEADY *goes.*] Fine thing to be letting rooms to every class of gouger and bowsey in the city.

PAT. Dirty thieves and whores the lot of them. Still, their money is clean enough.

MEG. It's not the whores I mind, it's the likes of that old whited sepulchre. That I don't like.

PAT. You don't mean Monsewer?

MEG. No I don't, I mean that old Mulleady geezer, though that old Monsewer is bad enough, giving out about the Republic and living in a brockel.

PAT. He doesn't know a thing about that; he thinks it's the War of Independence that's still going on.

MEG. He doesn't.

PAT. He does. He thinks all the people that come here are all Gaels and Republicans and patriots on the run.

MEG. The old idiot. He's here again.

MONSEWER. Patrick.

PAT. Commandant-General.

MONSEWER. As you were.

PAT. Thank you, Monsewer.

MONSEWER. I trust we may rely on the lads in the billet if anything should go wrong.

PAT. We may put our lives in their hands, Monsewer.

MEG. God help us.

MONSEWER. That's all I wanted to know. There seemed to be a bit of rumpus in here a minute ago.

PAT. Someone dropped something, sir.

MONSEWER. Bound to be a bit restless, I suppose, on a night like this.

PAT. It's the strain of battle, Commandant.

MONSEWER. Carry on. You've plenty of fodder in.

PAT. For the horses, Commandant?

MONSEWER. For the men, for the men.

PAT. Oh yes—I mean Monsewer—it's funny how I still can't get used to the foreign title. Even after all these years. I mean Monsewer.

MONSEWER. French for Mister, you know, Patrick.

PAT. I never did understand how you came by it, Commandant.

MONSEWER. I wanted no truck with the English titles, my man; as you know, for some time I refused to use their language altogether.

PAT. Yes indeed, sir. When Monsewer came here, Meg, he wouldn't talk anything but Irish.

MEG. Most people wouldn't know what he was saying, surely.

PAT. They did not. When he went on a tram car or a bus he had to have an interpreter with him so as the conductor would know where he wanted to get off.

MEG. Ah, the poor man.

MONSEWER. Mister and missus are English forms of address.

MEG. I know the Irish for missus, Monsewer. It's Ban, isn't it? Now if you'd said that, Monsewer, I'd have been with you.

MONSEWER. Ban in the English means woman. So if your husband's name was Murphy, you'd be called Ban Murphy, Murphy's woman. Not really in the best of taste, you know.

PAT. Do you see now, Meg? [*Aside to* MEG.] These high-up old ones couldn't stick that at all, it was a bit too Irish that was, so they called themselves "madame".

MONSEWER. Madame, a fitting mode of address for a daughter of Ireland. Oh, by the by, Patrick—a patriot of ours called Pigseye has just done six months for the cause. He's to billet here at our expense till the end of his days.

PAT. Yes, sir.

MONSEWER. Carry on. [*He goes.*]

PAT. The patriot Pigseye has just done six months for robbery with violence.

MEG. Don't talk to me about Pigseye. He's as mean as the grave. He knocked off a hundred gross of nylons from the Haute Couture warehouse and not one did he offer to a girl in the street. No Bejasus, not even to the one-legged girl in No. 8.

PAT. I'll get the rent off him or he'll reach the end of his days sooner than he expects.

MEG. Still, Monsewer meant well.

PAT. He's not a bad old skin, for an Englishman.

MEG. You what?

PAT. I said for an Englishman.

MEG. An Englishman, and him going round in his kilt playing his big Gaelic pipes all day.

PAT. He was born an Englishman and remained one for years. His father was a bishop.

MEG. His father was a bishop. I'm not sitting here listening to that class of immoral talk. His father a bishop indeed.

PAT [*impatiently*]. He was a Protestant bishop.

MEG. Ah well, of course it's different with them, isn't it?

PAT. Monsewer went to one of these big colleges in England, and he slept in one room with the King of England's son.

MEG. It wouldn't surprise me if he slept in one bed with him, his father being a bishop.

PAT. He had riches and every class of comfort you could wish for, till he found out he was an Irishman.

MEG. Aren't you after telling me he was an Englishman?

PAT. He was an Anglo-Irishman.

MEG. In the blessed name of God, what's that?

PAT. A Protestant with a horse.

MEG. And what do they do when they're out?

PAT. Well, an Anglo-Irishman only works at riding horses, you know, and drinking whisky, or reading double-meaning books in Irish at Trinity College.

MEG. I'm with you now; he wasn't born one, he became one.

PAT. He didn't become one—he was one—on his mother's side, and as he didn't like his father much he went with his mother's people—he became an Irishman.

MEG. How did he do that?

PAT. Well, there's not all that much difference. He started going to the Irish classes in the Gaelic League in Red Lion Passage and wearing a kilt and playing Gaelic football on Blackheath, but then he threw the hammer after the hatchet and acted like a true Irishman here.

MEG. He came over to live in Ireland.

PAT. He fought for Ireland. Where's that girl with me cigarettes?

MEG. I can't think where she's got to. She's been gone an hour now.

PAT. Well, give me a pint of stout.

MEG. I will an' all, and myself one too.

PAT. He came over to die for Ireland.

MEG. Sure, many's the time you've been telling me stories about the times you was active; Monsewer on the back of his white horse at the head of his regiment, the cross of Christ held high in his right hand like Brian Boru in the battle of Clontarf leading his men to war and glory. Didn't you tell me about the time he was a corporal down at Cork?

PAT. He was not a corporal, but a general.

MEG. What difference is it, corporal, general or admiral? I knew he was some sort of ral.

PAT. As a matter of fact, he was an old idiot.

MEG. He can't be such an idiot or they wouldn't be sending fellows in from the I.R.A. today, officers and all.

PAT. What are you talking about?

MEG. I mean that young fellow that was in here the other day.

PAT. How did you know he was an officer?

MEG. Sure they wouldn't send an ordinary Joe Soap to see Monsewer, would they? In any case, you don't think I'm such a fool as not to know what's cooking here, do you? I've got eyes in my head.

PAT. Keep your mouth shut and don't be comparing that little rat of a fellow that was in here yesterday to a soldier like Monsewer and myself.

MEG. Even if he is half mad?

PAT. He wasn't half mad the first time I saw him, nor a quarter mad, God bless him.

MEG. Amen, amen. What drove him half mad then?

PAT. The treaty.

MEG. What?

PAT. The treaty. Some of our leaders made an agreement to have no more fighting with England.

MEG. The traitors.

PAT. Sure, they sold the six counties and Irishmen were forced to swear an oath to the British Crown.

MEG. I don't know about the six counties, but I shouldn't think the swearing would come so hard on you.

PAT. Five years' hard fighting—nobody knows what it was like. Heavy and many is the good man was killed—and we had victory at last—till they signed that Curse of God Treaty in London.

MEG. Whatever made them do it?

PAT. Well, Lloyd George and Birkenhead made a fool of Michael Collins and he signed it.

MEG. He should have been shot.

PAT. He was.

MEG. Ah, the poor man.

PAT. He was a great soldier and fought well for the old cause all the same for five long years. We used to call him the Laughing Boy. We'll sing my song for him—

'Twas on an August morning, all in the morning hours,
I went to take the warming air all in the month of flowers,
And there I saw a maiden and heard her mournful cry,
Oh what will mend my broken heart, I've lost my laughing boy.

So strong, so wide and brave he was, I'll mourn his loss too sore
When thinking that we'll hear the laugh or springing step no more,
Ah, curse the time, and sad the loss my heart to crucify
That an Irish son, with a rebel gun, shot down my laughing boy.

Oh had he died by Pearse's side or in the G.P.O.
Killed by an English bullet from the rifle of the foe
Or forcibly fed while Ashe lay dead in the dungeons of Mountjoy,
I'd have cried with pride at the way he died, my own dear laughing boy.

My princely love, can ageless love do more than tell to you
Go raibh mile maith Agath, for all you tried to do.
For all you did and would have done, my enemies to destroy,
I'll praise your name and guard your fame, my own dear laughing boy.

PAT [*sighing*]. Ah sure, it's a great story!

MEG. It's better than the show that used to be on the television below in Tom English's Eagle Bar, "This is Your Life".

PAT. It was not the end of the story. Some of us didn't accept the treaty. We went out fighting again—and we were beat. But Monsewer was loyal to the old cause and I was loyal to Monsewer. So when the fighting was done we came back together to this old house.

MEG. This dirty old hole.

PAT. Yes, and a good hole it was for many a decent man on the run for twenty years after that.

MEG. Who the hell was still running twenty years after that?

PAT. All true Republicans who wouldn't accept the treaty. Cosgrave was hunting the Republicans, so they put de Valera in and he started hunting them too.

MEG. I see—says the blind man. Well carry on with the coffin, the corpse can walk.

PAT. In the end it was no paying game—hiding hunted Republicans, so we had to take in all sorts of scruffy lumpers to make the place pay. This noble old house which housed so many heroes was turned into a knocking shop. Still, I had you to help me.

MEG [*in tears*]. Oh you lousy bastard. The curse of God meet and melt you and your rotten lousy leg. You had me to help you, indeed. If I'm a whore itself, sure I'm a true patriot.

PAT. Ah sure and I know that, my dear. Now listen to me—sure you didn't think it was you I was talking about. Aren't we man and wife . . . nearly?

MEG. Yes, Pat, we are—well, nearly.

PAT. Sure I wasn't referring to you or meaning you at all, alana. I was talking about Ropeen and Colette, that pair of brasses, and the Mouse, Pigseye and Bobo. Nobody could deny that they're a pack of whores and thieves.

MEG. No indeed, that Colette anyway after what she done to the poor old Civil Servant out of the Ministry of . . .

PAT [*interrupting*]. Never mind that now.

MEG. Ah well now, Pat, it was no joke, and the poor old man on his knees at the bedside saying his prayers, to go robbing his money and him wearing nothing but his night-shirt, in the presence of Almighty God so to speak.

PAT. No, sure you couldn't blame me, darling, for anything I would call the like of her.

MEG. Certainly not I couldn't. Here's Princess Grace coming down now.

PAT. For Jasus' sake don't let on to any of them scruffs for what you know will be happening here tonight.

MEG. Mum's the word.

PRINCESS GRACE *enters with* RIO RITA.

PRINCESS GRACE. Isn't he marvellous?

PAT. Have you your rent?

PRINCESS GRACE. Of course, dear. I've never been at a loss yet, have I? You'll never guess how I got it this time. I hadn't been out five—

PAT. Never mind that now. Give me it. It's all one to me how you got it once you have it.

PRINCESS GRACE. There you are, Judas.

PAT. Thanks. [*Takes a book from his pocket.*] Now what's this your name is? I can't put down Princess Grace.

PRINCESS GRACE. No dear, that's only my name in religion.

MEG. Don't be giving out that talk about religion now.

PRINCESS GRACE. He's lovely, isn't he?

PAT. Here we are, week ending the twenty-second, received with thanks from John L. Sullivan.

PRINCESS GRACE [*simpering*]. That was my maiden name, darling. Oh, by the way, I've something to tell you. About that Mr. Mulleady. I think it's disgraceful. It certainly makes very little of you, Meg, and all the other girls in the house.

MEG. What are you talking about?

PRINCESS GRACE. It's about the fifth floor back, you know, Mr. Mulleady.

MEG. What about him?

PRINCESS GRACE. I wouldn't think much of myself if people brought strange women into the house anyway, and me a working girl.

MEG. What are you talking about.

PRINCESS GRACE. A strange woman, dear, not a woman of the house, an outsider. Three-quarters of an hour she's been in there and the noises—

PAT. What sort of a woman?

PRINCESS GRACE. A female woman.

MEG. The dirty, low degenerate old maniac, what does he take this house for? [*Calling*.] Mr. Mulleady!

MISS GILCHRIST *is heard singing*.

MEG. Mr. Mulleady!

MR. MULLEADY [*calling*]. Is that you, Mrs. M.?

MEG. Is it me? Who do you think it is? Come down to hell out of there at once, and bring that shameless bitch along with you.

PRINCESS GRACE [*to* PAT]. Here he comes with his airs and graces.

MR. MULLEADY. Did you call me, Mrs. M. dear? And what is it you'll be wanting?

MEG. If Mulleady is your name, I called you. And I called that low whore you have up in your room as well. I didn't call her by her name, because I don't know what it is, if she has one at all. [*Calls again.*] Come down here, you whore, whoever you are.

MR. MULLEADY. My dear Mrs. M., I beg of you, she might hear you.

MEG. Who's she when she's at home? What's she got that I haven't got, I'd like to know?

MR. MULLEADY. She is a lady.

MEG. More shame to her. And don't call me your dear Mrs. M. again nor your cheap Mrs. K. either.

MR. MULLEADY. I wouldn't dream of such a thing, nor would I dream of bringing—

MEG. Dream of what?

MR. MULLEADY. A—a—the type you mention into this house.

PAT. It'd only be coals to Newcastle.

MEG. Now, Mr. Mulleady, Mr. Mulleady sir, don't you know you could have got anything like that here? I'm surprised at you, so I am. God knows I've stood by you through thick and thin even when that man there was wanting to cast you out into the streets for the low-down dirty old lag that you are.

They run round room.

MR. MULLEADY. Mrs. M., must we bring that up? We are trying to forget the painful past.

MEG. Ran away with the Church funds, he did.

MR. MULLEADY. Mrs. M., please.

MEG. And that's not the worst of it.

MR. MULLEADY. Not in front of strangers, I beg of you.

PRINCESS GRACE. And he told me he was something in the city.

MR. MULLEADY. Be quiet. You—you wasp.

PRINCESS GRACE. Oh buzz.

MR. MULLEADY. Go away. Mrs. M., please say no more. I'm sorry, please—

MEG. Call down that brasstitute.

MR. MULLEADY. She's—

MEG. Get her down out of that.

MR. MULLEADY [*calls*]. Miss Gilchrist!

MISS GILCHRIST *is singing.*

MEG. Louder.

MR. MULLEADY. Miss Gilchrist!

MISS GILCHRIST. Yes, Mr. Mulleady.

MR. MULLEADY. Will you come down a minute, please?

MISS GILCHRIST. I haven't finished the first novena, Mr. Mulleady.

MEG. Never mind the—

MR. MULLEADY. Mrs. Meg. Please, I'll get her down. To-morrow is another day, Miss Gilchrist. If you'll put on your hat we'll go out and take the air.

MEG. "Put on her hat." I'll give her hat.

A humming is heard.

MISS GILCHRIST. I'm coming. [*She descends.*] Well, who are all those good people?

MR. MULLEADY. That's er—this is er—she's—Mrs. Meg, Miss Gilchrist, Miss Gil—

MEG. Gilchrist! In the name of Christ, what kind of a name is Gilchrist?

MISS GILCHRIST. It is an old Irish name. In its original form "Giolla Christ", the servant or gilly of Christ.

MEG. You're a quare ould gilly of Christ, you whore.

MISS GILCHRIST. I take insults in the name of our insulted Saviour.

MEG. You take anything you can get, like a good many more. You've been three hours up in Mr. Mulleady's room.

MR. MULLEADY. A quarter of an hour, Mrs. M.

MEG. Shut up.

MISS GILCHRIST. We were speaking of our souls.

MR. MULLEADY *and* MISS GILCHRIST *sing—"Our Souls, Our Souls."*

MEG. You can leave his soul alone, whatever about your own soul, you bloody bitch. And take yourself out of here, before I'm dug out of you.

MISS GILCHRIST. I will give you my prayers.

MEG. You can shove 'em up in your cathedral.

MISS GILCHRIST. I forgive you. You are a poor sinful person.

MEG. And you're a half-time whore.

PAT. Compliments pass when the quality meet.

MISS GILCHRIST. Eustace.

Everyone looks round sharply.

MR. MULLEADY. Yes—er—Miss Gilchrist.

MISS GILCHRIST. Come away. This is Sodom and Gomorrah.

MEG *grabs him.*

MR. MULLEADY. I can't, Miss Gilchrist. I haven't paid my rent.

MISS GILCHRIST. I will pray for you, Eustace; my umbrella, please.

MR. MULLEADY. Will you come back, Miss Gilchrist?

MISS GILCHRIST. Our Lord will give me strength. [*To* PRINCESS GRACE.] God go with you. [*She goes.*]

MR. MULLEADY [*after her*]. Evangelina! [*She turns, salutes and goes.*]

PAT. Ships that pass in the night.

MEG. Did you ever see anything like it in your life? And now are you going to ask for an explanation, or am I?

PAT. Leave me out of it. You brought him here in the first place.

MEG. So I did, God help me. And you take your face out of here, you simpering little get.

MR. MULLEADY *makes to go.*

Not you, him.

PRINCESS GRACE. Who told you what was going on in the first place? There's gratitude. I always knew what he was! The old eyebox!

MR. MULLEADY. Informer!

PRINCESS GRACE [*going*]. Oh spit!

MR. MULLEADY. Layabout.

PRINCESS GRACE. Thief! [*To audience.*] I think they're all a load of beasts. [*Goes.*]

MEG. Well?

MR. MULLEADY. All this fuss over nothing. Poor Miss G. came to talk to me about religion.

MEG. That kind is the worst kind. You can take it from me.

PAT. From one who knows.

MR. MULLEADY. I won't be restrained like this, I tell you. I must be free of your remonstrances, Mrs. M. You don't seem aware of my antecedents, my second cousin was a Kilkenny from Kilcock.

MEG. I'll cock you— Take this broom and sweep out your room, you whoremaster.

MR. MULLEADY. I will not be treated this way. [*Goes.*]

MEG [*chasing him*). Take that! And go and sweep your room.

PAT. If the performance is over I'd like a cigarette.

MEG. I sent the skivvy out for them an hour ago. God knows where she's got to on the way. Have a Gollywog.

PAT. What in Jasus' name is that?

MEG. It's a French cigarette. I got them off that young attaché case at the French Embassy—the one that thinks all Irishwomen are his mother.

PAT. I don't like the look of them. I'll wait for me twenty Afton. Meanwhile I'll sing that famous old song, "The Hound that Caught the Pubic Hare".

MEG. You're always announcing these songs, but you never sing them.

PAT. Well, there is one I sing sometimes.

PAT [*sings*].

> There's no place on earth like the world
> Just between you and me
> There's no place on earth like the world
> Acushla, astore and machree.

TERESA *runs in.*

PAT. Musha, a hundred thousand welcomes to you, my colleen.

TERESA [*out of breath*]. Your cigarettes, sir. . . .

MEG. You were a long time gone for them. Were you lost in the place?

TERESA. I was, nearly. Shall I get on with the beds, Meg?

MEG. Yes, you can.

PAT. There's no sir but Monsewer in this house, my girl.

TERESA. Yes, sir.

PAT. Call me Pat.

TERESA. Pat, sir— Oh, by the way, there's a man outside.

MEG. Is he coming in?

TERESA. Well, he's just looking.

PAT. Is he a policeman?

TERESA. Oh no, sir, he looks respectable.

PAT [*going in to look*]. Where is he now?

TERESA. He's there, sir Pat.

The I.R.A. MAN *is gazing up at the street.*

PAT. I can't see without my glasses. Has he a trench coat and a badge?

TERESA. He has, sir, how did you know?

MEG. He's a fortune teller.

TERESA. The badge says he only speaks Irish.

PAT. Begod, then him and me would have to use the deaf and dumb language, for the only bit of Irish I can say would get us both prosecuted. That badge makes me think he's an officer.

MEG. An officer?

TERESA. He has another to say he doesn't drink.

PAT. That makes him a higher officer.

MEG. Begod, keep him out of here.

PAT. He'll come in, in his own good time. Now, Teresa girl, you haven't been here long but you can be trusted to keep your mouth shut?

TERESA. Oh yes, I can, sir.

PAT. We'll be having someone staying here; you'll bring him his meals. Now if you don't tell a living sinner about it, you can stay here for the rest of your life.

MEG. Well, till she's married anyway.

TERESA. Oh thank you, sir, indeed I'm very happy here.

PAT. You're welcome!

TERESA. And I hope you'll be satisfied with my work.

PAT. I'll be satisfied if you'll do a bit more laughing and not be so serious.

TERESA. I've always been a very serious girl.

Sings "Open the Door Softly".

Open the door softly,
Shut it—keep out the draught,
For years and years, I've shed millions of tears,
And never but once have I laughed.

'Twas the time the holy picture fell,
And knocked my old granny cold,
While she knitted and sang an old Irish song,
'Twas by traitors poor Ulster was sold.

So open the window softly,
For Jaysus' sake hang the latch,
Come in and lie down and afterwards,
You can ask me what's the catch.

Before these foreign-born bastards, dear,
See you don't let yourself down.
We'll be the Lion and Unicorn,
My Rose unto your Crown.

MEG. Hasn't she got a nice voice, Pat?

PAT. Ah! that makes a nice picture; do you know what you look like, Meg?

MEG. Yes, a whore with a heart of gold; at least, that's what you'd say if you were drunk enough!

Enter THE OFFICER.
He reads list of defects—

OFFICER. House part of main block in street separated from rest by half-ruined house. Two exit doors, access to the roof by trap door.

PAT. All correct, sir.

OFFICER. Six flights of stairs including steps to basement, at present blocked by rubbish. Will you have that cleared, please?

PAT. Impossible, sir, there's no rubbish there. [*Ad lib. list of articles in cellar.*]

OFFICER. The cellar must be cleared. Will you check that, please? Who are these women? [*Hands him paper. Indicates that women must go. They leave.*]

PAT. Wait till I get me glasses. [*He fishes out a large monocle.*]

OFFICER [*striding up and down*]. You have food in sufficient for one day?

PAT. We have, sir; we always take care of the scoff.

OFFICER. May I see the toilet arrangements?

PAT. This way, sir. Mind your head as you go in.

THE OFFICER *returns almost immediately and walks to the window.*

MONSEWER [*putting his head around door*]. Are you the fellow from H.Q.? Righteo. Carry on.

OFFICER. Who the hell was that?

PAT. My mother.

OFFICER. Can we be serious?

PAT. Sir!

OFFICER. Sign that paper if the facts are correct.

PAT. All correct, sir.

OFFICER. Now your rent books, please, or a list of the tenants.

PAT. I can give you that easy. There's Bobo, Ropeen, Colette, the Mouse, Pigseye, Mulleady, Princess Grace, Rio Rita, Meg, the new girl, and myself.

OFFICER [PAT *fetches his note-book*]. I'll tell you the truth, if it was my doings there'd be no such thing as us coming here. I'd have nothing to do with the place, and the bad reputation it has all over the city.

PAT. Isn't it good enough for your prisoner?

OFFICER. It's not good enough for the Irish Republican Army.

PAT. Isn't it now?

OFFICER. Patrick Pearse said "To serve a cause which is splendid and holy, men must themselves be splendid and holy."

PAT. Are you splendid, or just holy? Haven't I seen you somewhere before? It couldn't be you that was after coming here one Saturday night . . .

OFFICER. It could not.

PAT. It could have been your brother, for he was the spitting image of you.

OFFICER. If any of us were caught here now or at any time, it's shamed before the world we'd be. Still, I see their reasons for choosing it too.

PAT. The place is so hot, it's cold.

OFFICER. The police wouldn't believe we'd touch it.

PAT. If we're all caught here, it's not the opinion of the world or the police will be upsetting us, but the opinion of the Military Court. But then I suppose it's all the same to you; you'll be a hero, will you not?

OFFICER. I hope that I could never betray my trust.

PAT. Ah yes, of course, you've not yet been in Mountjoy or the Curragh glasshouse.

OFFICER. I have not.

PAT. That's easily seen in you.

OFFICER. I assure you, my friend, I'm not afraid of Red-caps.

PAT. Take it from me, they're not the worst [*to audience*] though they're bastards anywhere and everywhere. No, your real trouble when you go to prison as a patriot, do you know what it will be?

OFFICER. The loss of liberty.

PAT. No, the other Irish patriots, in along with you. Which branch of the I.R.A. are you in?

OFFICER. There is only one branch of the Irish Republican Army.

PAT. I was in the I.R.A. in 1916, and in 1925 H.Q. sent me from Dublin to the County Kerry because the agricultural labourers were after taking over five thousand acres of an estate from Lord Trales. They had it all divided very nice and fair among themselves, and were ploughing and planting in great style. G.H.Q. gave orders that they were to get off the land, that the social question would be settled when we got the thirty-county Republic. The Kerrymen said they weren't greedy like. They didn't want the whole thirty-two counties to begin with, and their five thousand acres would do them for a start.

OFFICER. Those men were wrong on the social question.

PAT. Faith and I don't think it was questions they were interested in, at all, but answers. Anyway I agreed with them, and stopped there for six months training the local unit to take on the I.R.A., the Free State Army, aye, or the British Navy if it had come to it.

OFFICER. That was mutiny.

PAT. I know. When I came back to Dublin, I was court-martialled in my absence and sentenced to death in my absence, so I said they could shoot me in my absence. [*Pause.*]

OFFICER. Silence!

PAT. Sir!

OFFICER. I was sent here to do certain business. I would like to conclude that business.

PAT. Let us proceed, shall we, sir? When may we expect the prisoner?

OFFICER. Today.

PAT. What time?

OFFICER. Between nine and twelve.

PAT. Where is he now?

OFFICER. We haven't got him yet.

PAT. You haven't got a prisoner? Are you going down to Woolworths to buy one then?

OFFICER. I have no business telling you any more than has already been communicated to you.

PAT. Sure, I know that.

OFFICER. The arrangements are made for his reception. I will be here.

PAT. Well, the usual terms, rent in advance, please.

OFFICER. Is it looking for money you are?

PAT. What else? We're not a charity. Rent in advance.

OFFICER. I might have known what to expect. I know your reputation.

PAT. How did you hear of our little convent?

OFFICER. I do social work for the St. Vincent de Paul Society.

PAT. I always thought they were all ex-policemen. In the old days we wouldn't go near them.

OFFICER. In the old days there were Communists in the I.R.A.

PAT. There were, faith, and plenty of them. What of it!

OFFICER. The man that is most loyal to his faith is the one that will prove most loyal to the cause.

PAT. Have you your initials mixed up? Is it the F.B.I. or the I.R.A. that you are in?

OFFICER. If I didn't know that you were out in 1916 I'd think you were highly suspect.

PAT. Sir?

OFFICER. Well, at least you can't be an informer.

PAT. Ah, you're a shocking decent person. Could you give me a testimonial I could use in my election address if I wanted to get into the corporation? The rent, please!

OFFICER. I haven't got it on me.

PAT. Isn't it better for yourself that you pay me the rent? Then if we're caught you can disown me—say I only did it for money.

OFFICER. Thinking of your own skin.

PAT. I was thinking of the movement's great reputation. Four pounds, please.

OFFICER. I tell you I haven't got it on me.

PAT. Then get it. If you haven't got it by the time your man arrives, I'll throw the lot of you, prisoner and escort, out by the scruff of the neck into the street.

OFFICER [*going to his hidden gun*]. I wouldn't be too sure about that.

MEG [*at the door*]. Can we come in now, Pat?

PAT. What do you want?

MEG. We want to put the sheets on the bed.

OFFICER. Who are these women?

PAT. Sure it's only Meg and Teresa. Come in.

MEG *and* TERESA *make the bed.*

OFFICER [*sotto voce*]. Tell them to be quick about it.

PRINCESS GRACE [*calling as he comes down the stairs*]. Pat—Mr. Pat.

PAT. What is it?

PRINCESS GRACE. I've got the news on my portable—listen—it's still going on.

MEG. What's on? We don't want to hear any of your bloody old jazz screeching, we hear enough of that all day coming from your room.

PRINCESS GRACE. No, it's the news about that lovely young man, you know the one that they're going to be hanging in Belfast.

EVERYBODY. They're going to hang him? They really are?

PRINCESS GRACE. Quiet everybody, it's still on.

PAT. I can't make out a word it says on that thing.

MR. MULLEADY *has entered behind* PRINCESS GRACE.

PRINCESS GRACE *is listening to the radio*, MR. MULLEADY *is explaining what the news item said. While it continues* MR. MULLEADY *speaks.*

MR. MULLEADY. A young man, eighteen years of age—it was made on behalf of the Government of Northern Ireland.

PRINCESS GRACE. Shhhhh.

MR. MULLEADY. It's to be eight o'clock tomorrow morning. No reprieve. The Lord Lieutenant—final, I'm afraid.

PRINCESS GRACE. Shhhhh. I can't get it now. Eight o'clock tomorrow morning as arranged.

PAT. Turn the bloody thing off.

MEG. God help us all.

TERESA. The poor boy.

PRINCESS GRACE. Eight o'clock in the morning—think of it.

MEG. Ah sure, they might have mercy on him yet. Eighteen years of age—the poor boy.

OFFICER. Irishmen have been hanged by the Englishmen at eighteen years of age before this. Not only the Irish either —Cypriots, too.

PAT. Arabs and Jews.

MEG. Yes and what about them poor Indians and Africans? Have you heard of them? Same thing happened to them. But do you think Mr. de Valera could do something about this? I'm sure he could stop it if he wanted to.

OFFICER AND PAT [*together*]. Mr. de Valera. (*It's the first time they ever agreed about anything.*]

MEG. I always heard that Mr. de Valera was a wonderful man. They say he can speak seven languages.

PAT. It's a terrible pity that English or Irish are not among them, so as we'd know what he was saying in odd times.

PRINCESS GRACE [*who has been fiddling with his portable radio*]. Quiet everybody. Something's happened.

EVERYBODY [*asks*]. What?

PRINCESS GRACE [*continues*]. They've kidnapped an English soldier.

OFFICER. Turn the thing up so that we can hear it.

PRINCESS GRACE *turns the radio up and gets a blast of music. Then he turns it back and we hear a low mumble of static—he interprets.*

PRINCESS GRACE. So he was kidnapped, it said. What was that? From a dance, I think. Yes—three men jumped from a motor car—they . . . dragged the soldier . . . made off in fast speed in the direction of the border.

OFFICER. Turn it off. Patrick, get them out of here.

PAT. I can't do that just at the moment without making a show of ourselves.

OFFICER. Then come outside with me.

PAT *and the* OFFICER *go out.*

PRINCESS GRACE. Who's he?

MEG. He's the man come about the rent.

PRINCESS GRACE *turns music up on the radio then goes.*

MR. MULLEADY. The poor boy—in his lonely cell—waiting all night for the screw coming for him in the morning.

TERESA. It would break your heart to be thinking about him.

MR. MULLEADY. I know just how he feels.

MEG. How do you know?

MR. MULLEADY. Well, I was inside myself.

MEG. Oh, I see.

MR. MULLEADY. My downfall was the *Pall Mall Gazette* in 1919.

MEG. The what?

MR. MULLEADY. The *Pall Mall Gazette*. It's a magazine. I saw an advertisement in it—it was for an Insurance Company. I put all my savings into this company and in return I was to receive an annuity of twenty pounds a year. Of course, when the annuity was due the value of money had declined. I had sold my youth all for that miserable twenty pounds a year. As a result I borrowed the Church funds but I was found out and sent to prison. I broke my poor mother's heart.

MEG. Well, I never caused my mother any sorrow—for I never knew her.

MR. MULLEADY. How very sad—you never had a mother.

MEG. I never heard of any living person that didn't have a mother—though there's plenty that has no fathers. I had one, but I never saw her.

MR. MULLEADY. Now I'm sentenced for life to this religious mechanic.

MEG. Anyway, are you going to sit all night there moaning about mothers? Did you brush your room?

MR. MULLEADY. I did not.

MEG. Well, go out and get a bottle of stout for me. It's all right, tell him to put it on the slate—you might as well make yourself useful—Teresa and I have a lot to do yet, getting this place tidy for all and sundry.

MR. MULLEADY *goes.*

TERESA. There's some awful strange people in this house, aren't there, Meg?

MEG. There's some awful strange people in the world.

TERESA. I like that gentle young man—there was no-one like him in the convent.

MEG. Do you mean Princess Grace?

TERESA. Yes, isn't it a funny name?

MEG. How long have you been out of the convent?

TERESA. I've just had the one job I told you about with that family in Drumcondra.

MEG. Why did you leave there? Did you half-inch something?

TERESA. What did you say?

MEG. Did you half-inch something?

TERESA. I never stole anything in my whole life.

MEG. There's no need to go mad about it—I never stole anything either. The grand chances I had—ah, I was young and foolish that time. God doesn't give us these chances twice in a lifetime.

TERESA. It wasn't that, Meg; there was a clerical student in the house.

MEG. Ah well, as far as that's concerned, you'll be a lot safer here. Do the nuns know you left that job?

TERESA. Oh no, they mightn't be too satisfied with me.

MEG. Well, don't say anything to Pat; it doesn't do to tell men everything. Here he comes.

PAT *enters with* MONSEWER.

MEG. Oh, isn't it terrible, Pat; they are after refusing mercy to that poor boy in Belfast. He will be hanged tomorrow morning at eight o'clock.

TERESA. Wouldn't it break your heart to be thinking of him?

MONSEWER. It won't break my heart.

PAT [*aside*]. 'Course, it's not your neck they're breaking either.

MONSEWER. It does not make me unhappy. It does not make me unhappy, but proud. It makes me proud and happy to know that the old cause is not dead yet, and that there are still young men willing and ready to go out and die for Ireland.

PAT. I'd say that young man will be in the presence of the

Irish martyrs of eight hundred years ago a couple of minutes after eight tomorrow morning.

MONSEWER. He will. He will. With God's help, tomorrow morning he will be in the company of the heroes. It warms my heart to think of it.

MEG. Me life and yours.

MONSEWER. I would give all that I have in the wide world to stand in the place of that young man in Belfast Jail tomorrow morning. For Ireland's sake I would hang crucified in the town square.

PAT. Let's hope it would be a fine day for you.

MEG. Or you wouldn't get the crowd.

MONSEWER. I think he's very lucky.

PAT. It's a pity he didn't buy a sweepstake ticket. You were always a straight man, General, if I may call you by your Christian name. Well, all preparations are made for the guest.

MONSEWER. Good. Carry on. [*Exit.*]

PAT *exits, singing "Had he died by Pearse's side or in the G.P.O."*

TERESA. Wasn't that the ridiculous talk that old one had out of him about the boy being hung?

MEG. Well, Monsewer doesn't look at it like any ordinary person. Monsewer is very given to Ireland and to things of that sort.

TERESA. I think he's an old idiot.

MEG. An idiot? Monsewer was in all the biggest colleges of England, I'll have you know.

TERESA. It's all the same where he was. He is mad to say that the death of a young man made him happy.

MEG. Well, the boy himself said in court when they sentenced him to death that he was proud and happy to die for Ireland.

TERESA. He hasn't lived yet.

MEG. Have you?

TERESA. A girl of eighteen knows more than a boy of eighteen.

MEG [*sighs*]. They could easy do that. Poor lad. He gave no love to any, except to Ireland, and instead of breaking his heart for a girl, it was about the cause he was breaking it.

TERESA. Well, his white young neck will be broken tomorrow morning anyway.

MEG. Sure, we can't be thinking of it. It'd break our hearts. Let us have a bit of music. There's no need to mourn him before the time.

The hornpipe called "The Blackbird" is heard on the radio. They look at each other and TERESA *smiles. She goes out on the floor and dances to the music. She offers her hand to* MEG, *inviting her to join the dance.* MEG *comes out, slowly and shyly at first, but in the finish the two are dancing opposite each other, lively and gay.*

THE RADIO . . . *The Blackbird* . . .

The door opens right unknownst to the two girls dancing, and a young man in British Army khaki battledress stands in the door. TERESA *sees him first and it gives her a shock. She stops dancing.* MEG *follows* TERESA'*s gaze to the door and she stops.*

SOLDIER Don't stop. I like dancing.

OFFICER. Keep your mouth shut and get up there.

He is quite at ease and smiling. He comes in with the OFFICER *and another* MAN *behind him. They have their hands in the pockets of their raincoats.*

SOLDIER *sings:*

There's no place on earth like the world.
There's no place wherever you be,
There's no place on earth like the world,
That's straight up and take it from me.

Never throw stones at your mother,
You'll be sorry for it when she's dead,
Never throw stones at your mother,
Throw bricks at your father instead.

The South and the North Poles they are parted,
Perhaps it is all for the best,
Till the H-bomb will bring them together—
And there we will let matters rest.

ACT II

One door is guarded by the OFFICER, *the other by the* VOLUNTEER. *The* SOLDIER *walks up and down whistling to himself.*

SOLDIER [*plucking up courage*]. Hey! Hey!

There is no response. He whistles loudly. Both the OFFICER *and the* VOLUNTEER *poke their heads round the door at the same time.*

SOLDIER. HALT!

VOLUNTEER *halts.*

OFFICER. What's going on in here?

SOLDIER. Any chance of a cigarette?

OFFICER. Don't smoke.

VOLUNTEER *shakes his head.*

SOLDIER. Oh.

They go. He walks again.

VOLUNTEER. Hey!

SOLDIER. Yeah?

VOLUNTEER. You'll get a cup a tea in a minute.

SOLDIER. Smashing.

The SOLDIER *whistles to himself. Suddenly a shrill blast brings in the two heads again.*

OFFICER. Well, what's the matter now?

SOLDIER. Nothing.

OFFICER. What's all the noise about?

SOLDIER. I just thought that she might be bringing my tea in.

OFFICER. Who's she?

SOLDIER. The one we saw at first, you know; bit of all right, eh?

No response. They go.

OFFICER [*to* VOLUNTEER]. Keep him covered. I'll go and see how the tea's coming along.

PRINCESS GRACE, RIO RITA, MULLEADY *and* WHORES *appear and try to see the prisoner.*

PAT [*entering*]. Come on, out of here, you lot. You don't own the place.

PRINCESS GRACE. Why?

PAT. We're having the room fumigated. Out!

They go. PAT *calls* TERESA *in.*

Go on. Take it in to him now.

TERESA *goes into the room, with a tray.*

SOLDIER. Hallo. Cor, I was hoping I'd see you again.

TERESA. I was after bringing you a nice tea.

SOLDIER. Hey. I liked your dancing. The old foot-work.

TERESA. Thank you. [*She can't find a place for the tray.*]

SOLDIER. Going to have some with us?

TERESA. Don't stand there like an idiot. Don't you need it yourself? Your belly must be stuck to your back with hunger.

SOLDIER. Hey. Did you cook it for me yourself?

TERESA. Yes. You're lucky, Meg gave me two rashers.

SOLDIER. Good old Meg!

TERESA. She said you must have double the meal of a grown person because you have two jobs to do.

SOLDIER. What are they?

TERESA. To live and to improve, like all boys.

SOLDIER. Here. I'm older than you, I bet.

TERESA. I think you look like a boy.

SOLDIER. Look, I'm nearly nineteen.

TERESA. So am I.

SOLDIER. When were you born?

TERESA. January. Twenty-fifth of January. You?

SOLDIER. The eighteenth of August.

TERESA. So you see, I am older than you.

PAT *walks up and down outside. She looks out and he winks at her. She sits down.*

TERESA. What name do we call you?

SOLDIER. Tell me yours first.

TERESA. Teresa.

SOLDIER. Teresa! That's real Irish, ain't it? I'm a Leslie.

TERESA. A Leslie?

SOLDIER. Got a fag?

TERESA. A what?

SOLDIER. A cigarette.

TERESA. No, thank you. I don't smoke.

SOLDIER. No, I mean . . . for me. You couldn't get me one, could you?

TERESA. Wait a minute, I think I have one on me. Look, it's only a bit crushed, Pat gave it to me though he knows I don't smoke. Here!

SOLDIER. I suppose you couldn't get me a packet.

TERESA. I'll get you twenty Afton.

SOLDIER. Oh no. I mean . . . thanks, anyway. Ten'll do.

TERESA. You don't fancy the Irish cigarettes?

SOLDIER. What? The old Aftons? Take hundreds of them with me when I goes home on leave.

TERESA. You shall have twenty of them. After all, you have the night before you.

He looks around at the bed.

Are you looking for something?

SOLDIER. No. Yes, an ashtray.

TERESA. Under the bed?

SOLDIER [*blushing*]. Well, I might have been looking for the in and the out, mightn't I?

TERESA. The in and the out?

SOLDIER. Well, I'm a prisoner, ain't I?

TERESA. I'd better go. Oh, the tray; they'll be needing it.

SOLDIER. Will you be back?

TERESA. I may be. I only work here, you know.

TERESA *goes.*

SOLDIER [*to* VOLUNTEER]. Excuse me, mister, but—

VOLUNTEER. Don't keep bobbing about.

SOLDIER. I'd like to have a—you know!

PAT. What's he saying?

VOLUNTEER. He wants a—to go round the back, sir.

PAT. Well, he can, can't he, surely?

VOLUNTEER. No, sir. I'm in the same plight myself, and I can't move from this door for another hour yet.

PAT. Why don't you both go?

VOLUNTEER. We'll have to ask the officer.

PAT. Well, I'll call him. Sir! Are you there, sir?

The OFFICER *appears.* PAT *whispers to him.*

[*To* AUDIENCE.] A man wants to go round the back and it's a military secret.

OFFICER. Right! Attention! Fall in! [*To* PAT.] You in front! Quick march! Halt! Right! You two guard the door! Silence!

TERESA *comes in quickly with the cigarettes.*

TERESA. Leslie!

OFFICER. What are you doing here?

TERESA. Where is he?

OFFICER. What is this man to you?

TERESA. Nothing, sir. I was just bringing him his cigarettes, sir.

OFFICER. Give them to me.

TERESA. But they're his, sir; he gave me the money for them.

PAT [*off*]. Attention! Quick march! At the double! One man relieved, sir.

The three come marching back into the room.

VOLUNTEER. What about me?

OFFICER. Silence!

TERESA. Where has he been?

PAT. Doing a job that neither you nor me nor anyone else could do for him.

TERESA. Leslie, I got you—

OFFICER. That's enough. Get along with you! About your business.

He takes PAT *aside.*

OFFICER. Is that girl all right?

PAT. Now, now, you shouldn't have your mind on that sort of thing and you on duty—

OFFICER. I mean will she keep her mouth shut?

PAT. Sure now, you know what women are about these things. Did you have a bit last night? But I don't think she'd fancy you somehow.

OFFICER. I'm asking if she's to be trusted.

PAT. You mean would she help your man to beat it?

OFFICER. Yes.

PAT. She'd do nothing to bring the police to the house, I'm sure of that. And as for helping him to get away, if I've got eyes in my head, she's all for keeping him here. It seems they're getting along very well.

OFFICER. Yes. A bit too well for my liking.

PAT. Well, sir, she's passing the time for him. Isn't it better to have him well entertained, than roaring and bawling and looking for a fight? Sure, they looked like two little budgeriguards to me.

OFFICER. This is no laughing matter, you idiot.

PAT [*to* AUDIENCE]. You know, there are two sorts of gunmen, the earnest, religious-minded ones, like you, and the laughing boys.

OFFICER. Like you.

PAT. Well, you know in the time of the troubles it was always the laughing boys who were the most handy with a skit.

OFFICER. Why?

PAT. Because it's not a natural thing for a man with a sense of humour to be playing with firearms and fighting. There must be something the matter with him.

OFFICER. There must be something the matter with you, then.

PAT. Of course there is. Give him the bloody cigarettes.

The OFFICER *flaps them up and down in his hand, debating, when suddenly all the other characters rush on to the stage.*

MISS GILCHRIST. I heard them at the end of the street.

MEG. Have they gone past? Here they come.

PRINCESS GRACE. Look at 'em all. There's hundreds.

MEG. THOUSANDS!

PAT. What's going on? Yes, what's going on?

MEG. They're marching to the G.P.O. over the boy that's being hung tomorrow.

PAT. Oh sure, the procession.

TERESA. The poor boy, the poor boy.

They all come down to the footlights. The lights change so that you can only see their faces in spotlighting. The face of the SOLDIER *is picked out on the platform above. In the darkness the "Flowers of the Forest" is heard on the pipes.*

Sh! Here they come.

PAT [*as the pipes fade*]. There they go. It's like a funeral. Jim Larkin's funeral.

OFFICER. Plenty of police about.

MONSEWER. Plenty of banners. Another victim for occupied Ireland.

MEG. "England, the hangman of thousands. In Kenya, in Ireland, in Cyprus! In India! The World!"

MULLEADY. "Release the Belfast martyr!"

MEG. "We'll See Another Day When England Will Be That Low You Won't Be Able To Walk On Her!"

PRINCESS GRACE. "Eighteen Years of Age—in jail for Ireland!"—ah, the poor boy. Oh, the murdering bastards.

The faces watch the procession going.

SOLDIER. You know who they're talking about, don't you? 'Course all the papers twist it. That Irish fellow in Belfast Jail that's to be topped tomorrow morning. Did you read about him in the papers? We did. They was full of it where we were. Of course, most of our lads are National Servicemen, you know. I mean they're all about the same age as this young fellow that's going to be topped.

MEG. That's the end of it.

PAT. Ah well, thanks be to God it's not the way we all go.

MISS GILCHRIST. Is this the English boy? May I give him a little gift?

PAT. What is it?

MISS GILCHRIST. An article in a newspaper and as it's about his own Queen I thought he might like it.

OFFICER. What is it called?

MISS GILCHRIST. It is from the *Daily Express*. It is called "Within the Palace Walls". Here, I will read what it says on the cover. "Within the Palace Walls. So much is known of the Queen's life on the surface, so little about how her life is really run. But now this article has been written with the active help of the Queen's closest advisers."

SOLDIER. No thanks, ma'am, I don't go for that sort of mullarkey. Haven't you got something else?

MULLEADY. Evangelina!

MISS GILCHRIST. Who calls?

MULLEADY. Me! Me! Me! Me! Bookie! Please! Please!

MISS GILCHRIST. Well, if the boy doesn't want it.

MULLEADY. May I read on, please?

MISS GILCHRIST. Go on, Eustace.

MULLEADY. "Within the Palace Walls, because it is completely fresh, probing hitherto unreported aspects of her problems, this intriguing new serial lays before you the true pattern of the Queen's Life with understanding, intimacy, and detail." Oh! May I keep it, Miss Gilchrist?

PAT. Look at that, it's written by an Irishman—Dermot Morrah.

MEG. And she calls herself an Irishwoman, the silly old bitch.

MISS GILCHRIST. I have nothing against the Royal Family, I think they're lovely, especially Peter Townsend and Uffa Fox. I get every Sunday paper to follow them up. One paper contradicts another, so you put two and two together—and you might as well be sitting in the yacht with them. And there's that Mrs. Dale, she's a desperate woman, they even have an Irishman in it, a Mr. O'Malley, he keeps a hotel like you, Mr. Pat.

MULLEADY [*singing*].

I'll get this paper every day.
It will be my bible!

SOLDIER. Well, personally, mate, I'd sooner have the bleeding Bible. I read it once when I was on jankers.

MISS GILCHRIST. Is it true?

SOLDIER. It's blue, Mum.

MISS GILCHRIST. My favourite colour.

SOLDIER. You'd like it then, though the blue bits take a bit of sorting out from the dreary bits.

MISS GILCHRIST. May we sing to you?

MULLEADY *and* MISS GILCHRIST *sing "Nobody Loves You Like Yourself"*.

MULLEADY AND MISS GILCHRIST [*singing*].

You read the Bible in its golden pages,
You read those words, and talking much of love,

You read the works of Plato and the sages,
They tell of Hope, and Joy and Peace and Love,
But I'm afraid it's all a lot of nonsense,
About as true as leprechaun or elf,
You realize, when you want somebody,
That there is no one loves you like yourself.

I did my best to be a decent person,
I drove a tram for Murphy, in 'thirteen,
I failed to pass my medical for the Army,
But loyally tried to serve my King and Queen.
Through all the trouble times I was no traitor,
Even when the British smashed poor mother's delph,
And when they left, I was a loyal Free-stater,
But I know there is no one loves you like yourself.

I really think us lower middle-classes
Get thrown around just like snuff at a wake,
Employers take us for a set of asses,
The rough they sneer at all attempts we make,
To have nice manners and to speak correctly,
And in the end we're flung upon the shelf,
We have no unions, cost of living bonus,
It's plain to see that no one loves you like yourself.

Bows and curtseys; they go off.

PAT [*at end of song*]. Come on, that's enough of that. Get along with you.

TERESA [*entering, whispering*]. Leslie!

SOLDIER. Did you get my cigarettes?

TERESA. I gave them to that officer. Did he never pass them on to you?

SOLDIER. No.

TERESA [*she swears in Irish*].

SOLDIER. Now, now, now, no swearing. Anyway, you should never trust the officers.

There is a blast on MONSEWER'S *pipes.*

SOLDIER. What the hell's that?

TERESA. It's Monsewer practising his pipes. He's going to play a lament tomorrow morning, for the boy in Belfast.

SOLDIER. He's got a lot of practising to do, hasn't he?

TERESA. Don't joke about it.

SOLDIER. I'm not joking. I feel sorry for the poor fellow, but that won't help him, will it?

TERESA. He's one of your noble gentlemen, anyway; he went to college with your king.

SOLDIER. With who?

TERESA. Your king.

SOLDIER. We ain't got one.

TERESA. Maybe he's dead now, but you had one once.

SOLDIER. No, we got a Duke now.

TERESA. Anyway, he left your lot and came over and fought for Ireland anyway.

SOLDIER. What did he want to do that for? Was somebody doing something to Ireland?

TERESA. Wasn't England, for hundreds of years?

SOLDIER. That was donkeys years ago. Anyway, everybody was doing something to someone in those days.

TERESA. And what about today? What about that young man in Belfast Jail?

SOLDIER. Well, you know, you can't let blokes go round shooting at coppers. I don't fancy coppers much myself, but you've got to have law and order. And a copper couldn't even walk his beat if everyone who didn't like him started taking pot-shots at him.

TERESA. In the six counties the police walk the beat in tanks and armoured cars.

SOLDIER. Look, if he was an Englishman he'd be hanged just the same.

TERESA. It's because of the English being in Ireland that he fought.

SOLDIER. And what about the Irish being in London? Thousands of them. Nobody's doing anything to them. . . . 'Course, that's London. That's where we should be, down the 'dilly on a Saturday night.

TERESA. You're as bad as the Dublin people here; they think they're great.

SOLDIER. Don't you come from Dublin, Teresa?

TERESA. No, I don't.

SOLDIER. Country yokel, are you, Teresa?

TERESA. I was reared in the convent at Ballymahon.

SOLDIER. I was reared in the Old Kent Road.

TERESA. Is that where your father and mother live?

SOLDIER. I ain't got none.

TERESA. You're not an orphan, are you?

SOLDIER. Yes, that's right. I'm one of the little orphans of the storm.

TERESA. I don't believe you.

SOLDIER. Well, actually my old lady ran off with a Pole, not that you'd blame her if you knew my old man.

MONSEWER *enters playing bagpipes.*

SOLDIER. The only good thing about those pipes is they don't smell.

MONSEWER. That wasn't too good, was it, Patrick?

PAT. No, sir, it wasn't.

MONSEWER. Never mind. We'll get there. I'll have it by tomorrow morning.

PAT. Yes, sir.

MONSEWER. I'd like to see the prisoner a moment.

PAT. Certainly, sir. [*He enters room.*] Now then. You come down here. To attention! Stand by your bed.

MONSEWER. What's she doing here? Fraternizing?

PAT. No, sir, not at the moment. She's just remaking the bed.

MONSEWER. Now, you, my boy, what's your name?

SOLDIER. Williams, sir. Leslie A.

MONSEWER. Stationed at?

SOLDIER. Armagh, sir.

MONSEWER. Did you like it?

SOLDIER. No, sir. What a dump! Everything shuts at ten. The place is dead. You can't get a drink on Sunday. I can't think why they ever sent us there.

MONSEWER. You see, Patrick, morale is bad.

PAT. Dreadful, sir.

SOLDIER. Excuse me, sir, can I ask you a question?

MONSEWER. Go ahead.

SOLDIER. What are those pipes for?

MONSEWER. These? To play, of course. They are the instrument of a noble and ancient race.

SOLDIER. I see. I never could get the hang of all this race lark business myself; much too complicated.

MONSEWER. This race lark, as you call it, is when a lot of people have lived in the same place for a very long time.

SOLDIER. Then I reckon our old Sergeant Major must be a race. He's been living at the old depot for nearly forty years.

MONSEWER. What regiment are you with?

SOLDIER. R.E.M.E., sir.

MONSEWER. Ah, you mean the Royal Electrical and Mechanical Engineers, a very good regiment, very good indeed.

SOLDIER [*to* PAT]. You know he's the spitting image of our old Colonel back at the depot. Same face, same voice. Gorblimey, I reckon it is him.

MONSEWER. Focail . . .

SOLDIER. He a Free Hungarian or something?

MONSEWER. Focailelle.

SOLDIER. What's that, garlic?

PAT *gestures to him to shut up.*

MONSEWER. Has he come here to make a mockery of a civilization that was old in the days of the Greeks?

SOLDIER. Did he say Greek? I know a Greek bloke who runs a café down the Edgware Road, smashing scoff, only thing is it gets a bit greasy, but mind you, the rosy lee and holy ghost is marvellous. Best anywhere in London.

MONSEWER. Rosy Lee. What abomination is this?

SOLDIER. C. of E., guv.

PAT. Cockney humour, sir.

MONSEWER. You can't even speak the Queen's English.

PAT. He can't even speak his own English.

SOLDIER. I can make myself understood everywhere. Don't matter whether I'm in Brixton or Hampstead or anywhere.

MONSEWER. No background, no tradition, nothing.

SOLDIER. Oh yes I have. They gave us all that at the Boys' Home. Cricket, team spirit, fair play—we took all that.

MONSEWER. Did you play cricket?

SOLDIER. Yes, sir. Do you like a game?

MONSEWER. Yes.

SOLDIER. Mind you, I couldn't get on with it at the Boys' Home. They gave us two sets of stumps, you see, and I'd always been used to one, chalked up on the old wall at home.

MONSEWER. That's not cricket, my boy.

SOLDIER. Now there you are, you see. Now you're what I call a cricket person and I'm what I call a soccer person. There's where your race lark comes in.

MONSEWER. Ah, cricket, by jove that takes me back. Fetch the pianist, Patrick. Strange how this uncouth youth has brought back half-forgotten memories of summers long past.

He sings "The Captains and the Kings".

I remember in September
When the final stumps were drawn,
And the shouts of crowds now silent
And the boys to tea have gone.
Let us, oh Lord above us,
Still remember simple things
When all are dead who love us,
Oh, the captains and the kings,
When all are dead who love us,
Oh, the captains and the kings.

We have many goods for export
Christian ethics and old port,
But our greatest boast is that
The Anglo-Saxon is a sport.
When the darts game is finished
And the boys their game of rings

And the draughts and chess relinquished,
Oh the captains and the kings,
And the draughts and chess relinquished,
Oh, the captains and the kings.

Far away in dear old Cyprus,
Or in Kenya's dusty land,
Where all bear the white man's burden,
In many a strange land,
As we look across our shoulder,
In West Belfast the school bell rings,
And we sigh for dear old England,
And the captains and the kings,
And we sigh for dear old England,
And the captains and the kings.

In our dreams we see old Harrow,
And we hear the crow's loud caw,
At the flower show our big marrow
Takes the prize from Evelyn Waugh.
Cups of tea, or some dry sherry,
Vintage cars these simple things,
So let's drink up and be merry,
Oh, the captains and the kings,
So let's drink up and be merry,
Oh, the captains and the kings.

I stumbled in a nightmare,
All around Great Windsor Park,
And what do you think I found there
As I wandered in the dark.
'Twas an apple half-bitten,
And sweetest of all things,
Five baby teeth had written,
Of the captains and the kings,

Five baby teeth had written,
Of the captains and the kings.

By the moon that shines above us,
In the misty morn and night,
Let us cease to run ourselves down,
But praise God that we are white,
And better still are English,
Tea and toast and muffin rings,
Old ladies with stern faces,
And the captains and the kings,
Old ladies with stern faces,
And the captains and the kings.

Enter OFFICER. TERESA *hides under bed.*

PAT. Well, that's brought the show to a standstill.

OFFICER. Pat, get that old idiot out of here. Guard!

VOLUNTEER. Sir.

OFFICER. No one is to be allowed in here, do you understand? No ONE!

VOLUNTEER. Yes, sir. Sir, might I be relieved of my duties for just two minutes, sir, while I slip out the back . . .

OFFICER. No, certainly not. This place is like a rabbit warren with everyone skipping about.

MONSEWER. The laddie from headquarters. There you are!

OFFICER. Yes, here I am. I don't know quite how to put this, sir, but from now on I intend to have some discipline around here.

MONSEWER. Quite right, too.

OFFICER. I must ask you what you were doing in there?

MONSEWER. Inspecting the prisoner.

OFFICER. I'm afraid I must ask you to keep out of here.

MONSEWER. And I must ask you to remember my rank. I

know you're working under a strain at the moment, Captain, but—there's no need to treat me like an Empire Loyalist. You know where to find me when you need me, Patrick?

PAT. Very good sir.

MONSEWER. I'll be working on my plan. Chin up, sonny.

SOLDIER. Cheerio, sir.

OFFICER. Now, we've had enough of this nonsense. I'll check the room myself.

PAT. Yes, sir.

He sits on the bed and TERESA *yells.* PAT *coughs.*

SOLDIER. Can I ask you what you intend to do with me, guvnor?

OFFICER. Keep your mouth shut and no harm will come to you. Have you got everything you want?

SOLDIER. Oh yes, sir.

OFFICER. Right. Take over, Patrick. I'm going to the end of the street to check the other sentries.

PAT. Yes. Have you got the place well covered, sir?

OFFICER. Why?

PAT. It looks like rain.

OFFICER. No more tomfoolery, please.

Exit OFFICER. PAT *moves and stands outside the room.* TERESA *looks out from under the bed and calls* "Leslie."

SOLDIER. I'm not here. I've gone home.

TERESA. Have they gone?

SOLDIER. You wanted to stay with me, Teresa? Didn't you? Didn't you?

TERESA. No I didn't, I just didn't want him to see me. I'm going now.

SOLDIER. Don't go.

TERESA. Why?

SOLDIER. I—well, I like company.

TERESA. I shouldn't be here now; you heard what he said.

SOLDIER. Stay. I'll hide you if he comes back.

TERESA. Meg'll be wondering where I am.

SOLDIER. She told me she thought you was in the kitchen. Stay. Go on—stay and tell me a story—the Irish are great at that, aren't they?

TERESA. Well, not all of them—I'm not. I don't know any stories.

SOLDIER. Well, any story'll do. It doesn't have to be funny. It's just something to pass the time, ain't it?

TERESA. Yes. You've a long night ahead of you, and so has he.

SOLDIER. Who?

TERESA. You know, the boy in Belfast.

SOLDIER. He? Oh, don't start talking about that again, that'll spoil it.

TERESA. I'll tell you about when I was a girl in the convent.

SOLDIER. Yeah, that should be a bit of all right. Go on.

TERESA. Oh, it was the same as any other school, except you didn't go home—you played in a big yard which had a stone floor—you'd break your bones if you fell on it. But there was a big meadow outside the wall, and on Feast Days and holidays we were let out there. It was lovely. We were brought swimming a few times, too, but the nuns were awful careful, and if there was a man or a boy came within a mile of us we—well, we . . .

SOLDIER. Tell us, go on, go on, Teresa—after all we're grown-ups now, aren't we?

TERESA. We were not allowed to take off our clothes at all. You see, Leslie, even when we had our baths on Saturday nights they put shifts on the girls, even the little ones four or five years old.

SOLDIER. Did they?

TERESA. What did you have?

SOLDIER. Oh no, we never had anything like that. I mean, in our place we had all showers and we were sloshing water over each other and blokes shouting and screeching and making a row—it was smashing. Best night of the week, it was.

TERESA. Our best time was the procession we had for the Blessed Virgin on May Day—

SOLDIER. Procession for who?

TERESA. Shame on you, the Blessed Virgin. Anyone would think you were a Protestant.

SOLDIER. I am, girl.

TERESA. Oh, excuse me.

SOLDIER. That's all right. Never think about it myself.

TERESA. And anyway, on May Day we had this big feast.

SOLDIER. Was the scoff good?

TERESA. The . . . what?

SOLDIER. The grub! You don't understand what I'm talking about half the time, you know.

TERESA. Are you listening to me? Anyway, we had this procession, and I was with the mixed infants.

SOLDIER. What's a mixed infant?

TERESA. A little boy or girl under five years old. They were called mixed infants because until that time the boys and girls were mixed together.

SOLDIER. I wish I'd been a mixed infant.

TERESA. Do you want to hear my story? When the boys were six they were sent to the big boys' orphanage.

SOLDIER. You mean this place you were in was all orphans? Do you, Teresa? Were you one?

TERESA. I told you I was.

SOLDIER. No you didn't.

TERESA. Yes I did.

SOLDIER. Well, shake on it anyway.

They shake hands.

TERESA. I didn't believe your story.

SOLDIER. Well, it's true. Anyway, never mind. Tell us about this mixed infant job.

TERESA. He was on his own and he was crying like the rain. His father was dead, but his mother had run away. All the other boys and girls were laughing and shouting, but this one boy was on his own and nothing would stop him. So do you know what I did? I made a crown of daisies and a daisy chain to put round his neck and told him he was the King of the May. He forgot everything except that he was King of the May.

SOLDIER. Would you do that for me if I was a mixed infant?

TERESA. There's a clock striking somewhere in the city.

SOLDIER. I wonder what time it is?

TERESA. I don't know.

The bagpipes are heard.

SOLDIER. Will you give me a picture of yourself, Teresa?

TERESA. What for?

SOLDIER. I'd like to take it with me. I mean, they might take me away in the night and I might never see you again.

TERESA. Besides, I'm not Marilyn Monroe or Jayne Mansfield.

SOLDIER. Who wants a picture of them? They're all old.

TERESA. I haven't got a picture.

She pulls out a medal which she has round her neck.

SOLDIER. What's that?

TERESA. It's a medal.

SOLDIER. I'm doing all right, ain't I? In the army nine months and I get a medal.

TERESA. It's not that kind of medal.

She gives it him.

SOLDIER. It looks like you.

TERESA. Leslie! No, it's . . .

SOLDIER. Oh, it's that lady of yours.

TERESA. Yes, it's God's mother. She's the mother of everyone in the world, too. Will you wear it round your neck?

SOLDIER. If you'll put it on, Teresa.

She does. He tries to kiss her.

TERESA. Leslie! Don't.

SOLDIER. Now don't give me that old bull. Let's pretend we're on the films where all I have to say is "Let me", and all you have to say is—"Yes".

Music.

Come on, Teresa.

She is shy but he pulls her down towards the footlights and they sing and dance. The song is "I Will Give you a Golden Ball". On the last verse they walk towards the bed. Quick Blackout.

TERESA [*sings*].

I will give you a golden ball,
To hop with the children in the hall,
If you'll marry, marry, marry,
If you'll marry me.

SOLDIER [*sings*].

I will give you the keys of my chest,
And all the money that I possess,
If you'll marry, marry, marry,
If you'll marry me.

TERESA [*sings*].

I will give you a watch and chain,
To show the children in the lane,
If you'll marry, marry, marry,
If you'll marry me.

SOLDIER [*sings*].

I will give you coins of gold,
And as much and more as your hands can hold,
If you'll marry, marry, marry,
If you'll marry me.

TERESA [*sings*].

I will bake you a big pork pie,
And hide you till the cops go by,
If you'll marry, marry, marry,
If you'll marry me.

BOTH [*sing*].

But first I think that we should see
If we fit each other. Yes, I agree.

They lie on the bed. MISS GILCHRIST *runs on and into a spot.*

MISS GILCHRIST. They're away. My music, please.

She sings "Only a Box of Matches".

MISS GILCHRIST [*sings*].

Only a box of matches
I send, dear mother, to thee—
Only a box of matches
Across the Irish Sea.

I met with a Gaelic pawnbroker,
From Killarney's waterfalls,
In sobs he cried, "I wish I'd died;
The Saxons have stolen my balls."

MISS GILCHRIST *exits.* MEG *is heard calling.*

MEG. Teresa! Teresa!

VOLUNTEER. You can't go in there. Sir! [OFFICER *enters.*]

OFFICER. Yes.

VOLUNTEER. There's a woman trying to get in to him.

OFFICER. You can't go in there. Security forbids it.

VOLUNTEER. Common decency forbids it. He might not have his trousers on.

MEG. Auah, do you think I've never seen a man with his trousers off before?

OFFICER. I'd be surprised if you'd ever seen one with them on.

MEG. Thanks.

VOLUNTEER. He's a decent boy, for all he's a British soldier.

MEG. Ah, there's many a good heart beats under a khaki tunic.

VOLUNTEER. There's something in that. My own father was in the Royal Irish Rifles.

OFFICER. Mine was in the Inniskillings.

MEG. And mine was a parish priest.

OFFICER. God forgive you, woman. After saying that, I won't let you in at all.

MEG. Oh, I'm not that particular. I wasn't thinking of going in in the first place, but was going about my business till he stopped me.

PAT. Auah, let her go in, officer, just for a second. It'll cheer the poor boy up a bit.

OFFICER. I don't think we should. He's in our care and we're morally responsible for his spiritual welfare.

VOLUNTEER. Well, only in a temporal way, sir.

MEG. I only wanted to see him in a temporal way.

OFFICER [*to* VOLUNTEER]. Jesus, Mary and Joseph, but it would be a terrible thing for him to die with a sin of impurity on his—

SOLDIER [*running down into a spotlight*]. What's all this talk about dying? Die! Who's going to die?

MEG. We're all going to die, but not before Christmas we hope.

PAT. Now look what you've done. You'll have to let her in now. You should have been more discreet, surely.

OFFICER. Two minutes then.

The OFFICER *and the* VOLUNTEER *move away. Lights up on the room.* TERESA *stands by the bed, frightened.*

MEG. She's there, she's been there all the time.

TERESA. I just came in to do the dusting, Meg.

She sits on the bed and turns from them.

MEG. What's wrong with a bit of comfort on a dark night?

SOLDIER. Please, mum, what are they going to do with me?

MEG. You can take your hand off my knee.

SOLDIER. Sorry, mum.

MEG. I keep that for my business.

SOLDIER. Will you go out and ask those blokes why they pinched me? I don't think they know themselves.

MEG. Maybe they don't know, maybe a lot of people don't know . . . or maybe they've forgotten . . .

SOLDIER. I don't quite see what you mean.

MEG. You can't forget some things.

SOLDIER. Forget?

MEG. In Russell Street, in Dublin, right next to where I was born, the British turned a tank and fired shells into people's homes.

SOLDIER. I suppose it was war, missus.

MEG. Yes, it was war. Do you know who it was against?

SOLDIER. No, missus.

MEG. Old men and women, the bedridden and the cripples, the mothers with their infants.

SOLDIER. Why them?

MEG. Everybody that was able to move had run away.

SOLDIER. That was hard luck, missus.

MEG. In one room they found an old woman, her son's helmet and gas mask were still hanging on the wall. He had died fighting on the Somme.

SOLDIER. I don't know nothing about it, lady.

MEG. Would you like to hear more? Then listen.

She sings the song "Who Fears to Speak of Easter Week".

MEG [*sings*].

Who fears to speak of Easter Week,
That week of famed renown,
When the boys in green went out to fight,
The forces of the Crown.

With Mausers bold, and hearts of gold,
The Red Countess dressed in green,
And high above the G.P.O.
The rebel flag was seen.

Then came ten thousand khaki coats,
Our rebel boys to kill,

Before they reached O'Connell Street,
Of fight they got their fill.

They had machine guns and artillery,
And cannon in galore,
But it wasn't our fault that e'er one
Got back to England's shore.

For six long days we held them off,
At odds of ten to one,
And through our lines they could not pass,
For all their heavy guns.

And deadly poisoned gas they used,
To try and crush Sinn Fein,
And burnt our Irish capital,
Like the Germans did Louvain.

They shot our leaders in a jail,
Without a trial they say,
They murdered women and children,
Who in their cellars lay.

And dug their grave with gun and spade,
To hide them from our view,
Because they could neither kill nor catch,
The rebel so bold and true.

The author should have sung that one.

PAT. That is if the bleeding thing has an author.

SOLDIER. He doesn't mind coming over here and taking our money.

OFFICER. Be Jesus, wait till he comes home. We'll give him making fun of the movement.

SOLDIER. He's too bleeding anti-British.

OFFICER. Too anti-Irish you mean.

MEG. Ah, he'd sell his country for a pint.

PAT. And put up his hands and thank the Almighty God that he had a country to sell.

SOLDIER. Author, author.

MONSEWER. Author!

PAT. He might as well show up; it's his only bleeding chance of getting a curtain call. A lot he cares.

Rock and Roll. Everybody dances. MUSICIAN *enters.*

MUSICIAN. Hey, Leslie!

SOLDIER. What?

MUSICIAN. Have you seen this?

SOLDIER. Throw it down.

He throws a newspaper on to the stage.

TERESA. What is it?

SOLDIER. The evening paper, isn't it? [*He reads.*] "The Government of Northern Ireland have issued a statement that they cannot find a reason for granting a reprieve in the case of the condemned youth." Here! I've got my name in the papers. 'Private Leslie Alan Williams', that's me! Look at that!

PAT. You want to read a bit further.

MULLEADY. Yes, read on—

MISS GILCHRIST. I'm afraid it's possible—it's likely—that you'll be shot.

SOLDIER. Who are you?

MISS GILCHRIST. I am a sociable worker. Have you your testament?

SOLDIER. I hope so.

MISS GILCHRIST. He is an exile, poor lad. I feel for him, like a mother.

Begins to sing, "Only a Box of Matches, I send, Dear Mother, to Thee".

SOLDIER. Shut up, this is serious. [*Reads.*] "In a statement today delivered to all newspaper offices and press agencies . . . he has been taken as a hostage . . . " that's me, a hostage! "If . . . executed . . . the Irish Republican Army declare that Private Leslie Alan Willams will be shot . . . will be shot . . . as a reprisal". [*Turns to the others.*] Does it really mean they're going to shoot me?

MULLEADY. I'm afraid so.

SOLDIER. Why?

MONSEWER. You're the hostage.

SOLDIER. I've done nothing wrong.

OFFICER. It's war.

SOLDIER. Would none of you let me free?

They all look at him.

Well, you crowd of bleeding— Give me some music, please.

He sings "I am a Happy English Lad".

I am a happy English lad
I love my royalty
And if they were short a penny on a packet of fags,
Now they'd only have to ask me.

I love old England in the east
I love her in the west
From Jordan's streams to Derry's Walls,
I love old England best.

I love my dear old Notting Hill
Wherever I may roam,
But I wish those bleeding Nigger-boys
Were kicked out and put back home.

CURTAIN

ACT III

PAT, MISS GILCHRIST *and* MEG *are sitting drinking. The* VOLUNTEER *and the* OFFICER *are standing ground over* LESLIE.

PAT [*sings,* MISS GILCHRIST *joining in with him.*]

> On the fifteenth day of November,
> Just outside the town of Macroom,
> The 'Tans in their big Crossley tenders,
> Came roaring along to their doom.

MEG. Shut up, the two of you, or you'll have that Holy Joe down on us.

PAT. Who are you talking about?

MEG. That I.R.A. general, or whatever he is.

PAT. Him a general—in the old days we wouldn't have had him as a batman. He's no more than a messenger anyway. Have some whisky, Miss Gilchrist?

MISS GILCHRIST. Oh no, thank you, Mr. Pat.

MEG. She doesn't want it.

PAT. Get it down!

MEG. I heard they're all generals nowadays.

PAT. Like their mothers before them. You are speaking to a man who was a captain at the time of the troubles, Miss Gilchrist.

MEG. Fine bloody captain he was.

MISS GILCHRIST. Really.

PAT. Captain of "E" Company, second battalion, Dublin Brigade. Monsewer was the commandant.

MEG. "E" Company, who are they?

PAT. You've heard of A B C D E, I suppose?

MEG. Certainly I have.

PAT. Well!

MISS GILCHRIST. Wasn't that nice! It must be a lovely thing to be a captain.

PAT. Will you let me get on with my story?

MEG. I defy anyone to stop you.

PAT. Leslie, it was in Russell Street in Dublin.

MEG. I've already told him.

PAT. Give us a bloody drink.

MEG. Get it yourself.

MISS GILCHRIST. Please go on.

PAT. Oh well, give us a drink. [*They drink.*] It was at Mullingar, on the field of battle, that I lost my leg.

MEG. You told me it was at Cork.

PAT. No matter what I told you, it was at Mullingar, in the Civil War.

MISS GILCHRIST. Well, if that's the kind of war you call a Civil War, I wouldn't like to see an uncivil one!

PAT. What a battle! The fight went on for three days without cease.

MISS GILCHRIST. And what happened to your poor left foot, Mr. Pat?

PAT. It wasn't me left foot, but me right foot. Don't you know your left foot from your right? Don't you know how to make the sign of the cross?

MISS GILCHRIST. I do, thank you, but I don't make it with my feet.

PAT. What does it matter, left or right? There were good men lost on both sides. Ah, it was a savage and barbarous battle, and they had Lewis guns, Thompsons, land mines. All we had were rifles and revolvers. The town was nothing but red fire and black smoke and the dead piled high on the roads.

MEG. You told me there was only one man killed.

PAT. I told you that?

MEG. And he was the County Surveyor out measuring the road and not interfering with politics one way or another.

PAT. You're a liar.

MEG. You told me that both sides claimed him for their own when the fighting was over—I've seen the Celtic crosses on either side of the road, where they put up memorials to him.

PAT. It's all the same what I told you.

MEG. That's your story when you're drunk, anyway. Of course, like every other man, that's the only time you tell the truth.

PAT. Have you finished?

MEG. No! Begod, if whisky and beer were at pre-war prices the Father of Lies would be out of a job.

PAT. I lost me leg anyway, didn't I? Did I or did I not?

MEG. You lost the use of it, I know that.

MISS GILCHRIST. These little lovers' quarrels!

MEG. You keep out of it, you silly old get.

PAT. I lost me leg anyway, and these white-faced loons with their trench coats, berets and teetotal badges have no right to call themselves members of the I.R.A.

MISS GILCHRIST. They're only lads.

MEG. He begrudges them their bit of sport now he's old and beat himself.

PAT. What sport is there in that dreary loon we have round here?

MEG. They've as much right to their drilling and marching, their revolvers and generals and sacrifices and white horses and wounds and last dying words and glory as you had.

PAT. I'm not saying they haven't, did I?

VOLUNTEER. Oh, yes, you did, Pat.

MISS GILCHRIST. I heard you distinctly.

MEG. Weren't you young yourself once?

PAT. That's the way they talk to you.

MISS GILCHRIST. I always say that a general and a bit of shooting makes you forget your troubles.

MEG. Sure, it takes your mind off the cost of living.

MISS GILCHRIST. A poor heart it is that never rejoices.

PAT. You keep out of this, Leslie. Watch him, Feargus. Anyway, they've no right to be going up to the border and kidnapping—

They all look round at LESLIE.

MEG. They have as much right to leave their legs and feet up in the border as you had to leave yours at Mullingar or Cork or wherever it was. Sit down, you shadow of a whore's ghost, and let's have a drink in peace. [*They drink.*]

MISS GILCHRIST *takes a drink to* LESLIE.

VOLUNTEER. You've been warned before.

PAT [*to* MISS GILCHRIST]. Move away. You're coming on to be making smart remarks like that to a poor cripple man that never harmed anyone in his life.

MEG. Away with you.

PAT. Let alone the years I did in Mountjoy, incarcerated with the other Irish patriots, God help me.

MEG. Ah, Mountjoy and the Curragh Camp were universities for the like of you. But I'll tell you one thing and that's not two, the day you gave up work to run this house for Monsewer, and entertain the likes of her, you became a butler—a Republican butler, a half-red footman —a Sinn Fein skivvy—

MISS GILCHRIST. What a rough-tongued person.

PAT. Go on, abuse me—your own husband that took you off the streets on a Sunday morning, when there wasn't a pub open in the city.

MEG. Go and get a mass said for yourself. The only love you had you kept for Mother Ireland and leaving honest employment.

PAT. Why do you stop with me so?

MEG. God knows.

SOLDIER *sings to himself.* MISS GILCHRIST *joins in.*

MISS GILCHRIST. Do you hear the poor lamb, keening to himself? The exiled boy! Ochone! Ochone! And it's a coffin of white planks they'll be bringing him before long. Ochone! Ochone!

MEG. What language is that she's talking?

PAT. Italian. Be quiet, you queer old bird—have a drink!

MISS GILCHRIST. Oh, Mister Pat, God increase you.

SOLDIER [*sings*]. Rule Britannia, Britannia rules the waves.

PAT. Move over there if you're going to keep on moaning. [*To* SOLDIER] Hey!

MEG. I don't want her here.

SOLDIER. Yes!

PAT. If you must sing, sing something modern. Not Rule Britannia.

SOLDIER *is silent.*

You know, something cheerful and up to date.

SOLDIER. I can't think of anything.

VOLUNTEER. Then shut up.

MISS GILCHRIST. I know what it is to be an exile. Dublin is not my home.

MEG. That's one thing in its favour.

MISS GILCHRIST. I came here to run a house, Mr. Pat.

MEG. I told you what she was.

MISS GILCHRIST. It was in a very respectable district, you know, and we only took in clerical students. They were lovely boys, much more satisfactory than the medical students.

PAT. Ah yes, the medicals is more for the beer.

MISS GILCHRIST. Of course, my boys had renounced the demon drink. Being students of Divinity, they had better things to do.

MEG. What things?

PAT. Now, Meg! You know what they go in for, reading all about— "This one lay with that one", and "Mat begat Pat", and that old fellow lying with his daughters—

MEG. And getting the best of eating and drinking, too. It's a wonder they're anyway controllable at all.

MISS GILCHRIST. Sometimes they were not. Ah, life has its bitter memories.

PAT. Have a drink.

MISS GILCHRIST [*crying*]. Thank you. Since then I have had recourse to good works. Recalling the sinner, salvaging his soul.

MEG. We'll leave his soul out of it, whatever about your own, or I'll set fire to you.

MISS GILCHRIST. Our Blessed Lord said, "Every cripple has his own way of walking, so long as they don't cause strikes, rob, steal, or run down General Franco." Those are my principles.

MEG. Your principle is nothing but a pimp.

MISS GILCHRIST. To whom are you referring?

MEG. That creeping Jesus in the fifth floor back.

MISS GILCHRIST. Oh, you mean Mr. Mulleady?

MEG. I do.

MISS GILCHRIST. But he is a fonctionnaire.

MEG. Is that what they call it nowadays?

MISS GILCHRIST. I strove to save him, together we wrestled—against the Devil; but now I am more interested in this soldier's soul. [*Sings.*] I love my fellow creatures.

MEG. Leave that soldier's soul alone.

PAT. Leave him alone, he's too young for you.

MISS GILCHRIST. I'm as pure as the driven snow.

MEG. You weren't driven far enough.

PAT. Hey, Feargus.

VOLUNTEER. Captain.

PAT. Have a drink.

VOLUNTEER. Thanks!

PAT. Give him one as well.

SOLDIER. Here, it's all very well you coming the old acid and giving me all this old buck about nothing happening to me, but I'm not a complete bloody fool, you know.

PAT. Drink your beer.

SOLDIER. What have I ever done to you that you should shoot me?

PAT. What have you ever done for us? I'll tell you a little story. In the time of the famine, when our people were dying here like flies and your old Queen, Victoria was her name, she sends a five pound note to the famine fund, and just so they won't misunderstand her and take her for a rebel or something, she sends by the same post five pounds to the Battersea Dog's Home. Now you just think about that.

MEG. Good God, Pat, that was when Moses was in the Fire Brigade.

PAT. Let him think about that.

MISS GILCHRIST. They might have given us this island that we live on for ourselves.

SOLDIER. Can I ask you one thing, man to man? Why didn't they tell me why they took me?

PAT. Didn't they?

SOLDIER. No.

PAT. Well, there's a war going on in the North of Ireland. You were a soldier. You were captured.

SOLDIER. All right, so I'm captured. So I'm a prisoner of war.

PAT. Yes.

SOLDIER. Well, you can't shoot a prisoner of war!

PAT. Agreed! Who said anything about shooting?

SOLDIER. What about that announcement in the papers?

PAT. Bluff. Haven't you everything you could wish for? A bottle of stout, a new girl friend bringing you every class of comfort.

SOLDIER. Yes, till that bloke in Belfast is topped in the morning, then it'll be curtains for poor old Williams and I'm due for a week-end's leave an' all.

PAT. It's all bluff, propaganda! All they'll do is hold you for a few days.

MEG. And they might give him a last-minute reprieve.

SOLDIER. Who, me?

MEG. The boy in Belfast Jail, poor lad.

SOLDIER. Some hopes of that.

PAT. The British Government may be thinking twice about it now that they know we've got you.

VOLUNTEER. They know that if the Belfast martyr dies, their own man here will be plugged.

SOLDIER. And plug you!

PAT [*to* VOLUNTEER]. Be quiet, idiot, look how you've upset him! Take no notice of his nonsense.

SOLDIER. You're as barmy as him if you think that what's happening to Private Leslie Williams is upsetting the British Government. I suppose you think they're all sitting round in their West End clubs with handkerchiefs to their eyes, dropping tears into their double-whiskies. Yeah, I can just see it, the old Secretary of State for War waking his missus up in the night, "Oh, Isabel Cynthia," he'll say, "I can't get a wink of sleep wondering what's happening to that poor bleeder, Williams."

MISS GILCHRIST *cries.*

MISS GILCHRIST. Poor boy! Do you know, I think they ought to put his story in the *News of the World.* Ah, we'll be seeing you on the telly yet. Yes, he'll be famous like that Diana Dorn—or the other one who cut up his victim and threw the bits out of an aeroplane. Now, he has a serial running somewhere.

SOLDIER. I always heard the Irish were barmy. But that's going it, that is.

PAT. Eh, let's have a drink. [*Calls.*] Feargus!

VOLUNTEER. Sir! I can't leave my post.

SOLDIER. Here, mum, listen—

PAT [*to* LESLIE]. Now, you stay where you are. I'm going to fix you. Here, hold this. [*Gives him a bottle.*] Now, I'm going to draw a circle round you, see, like that. Now you move outside that and you're a dead man. Have you got that?

MISS GILCHRIST [*sings*].

> Just say there is no other
> To take the place of mother,
> And kiss her dear sweet lips for me—

SOLDIER [*moving out of circle*]. Hey.

PAT. Yes! Now, I told you.

SOLDIER. I bet that fellow in Belfast wouldn't want me to be plugged.

PAT. Certainly he wouldn't.

SOLDIER [*moving out*]. What good's it going to do him?

PAT. Inside! That's right! Sure and it won't do him any good.

MEG. When the boy's dead, what good would it be to croak this one? It wouldn't bring the other back to life now, would it?

SOLDIER. What a caper! I'm just walking out of a dance hall—

PAT. Walk in.

SOLDIER [*back inside*]. Then this geezer nabs me. "What do you want?" I says. "Information," he says. "I ain't got no information," I says, "apart from me name and number and the addresses of the girls who work in the N.A.A.F.I." "Right," says this bloke, "we're taking you to Dublin; our Intelligence men want to see you."

PAT. "Intelligence!" Holy Jesus, wait till you meet 'em. This fellow here's an Einstein compared to 'em.

SOLDIER. Well, when will I be meeting 'em?

PAT. They'll be coming tomorrow morning to ask you a few questions.

SOLDIER. Yes, my last wishes, I suppose!

PAT. I've told you before not to be such an idiot.

VOLUNTEER. He's told you.

MISS GILCHRIST [*sings*].

> I have no mother to break her heart
> I have no father to take my part.

PAT. Ah, don't be tormenting the life out of me with your moaning, woman. Sit up there in that circle. Leslie, come and sit here. That old idiot would put years on you.

MISS GILCHRIST [*as she goes*]. I'll have you know I had my voice trained by an electrocutionist.

MEG. It sounds like it.

VOLUNTEER. It's neither this nor that, commandant, but if you're taking charge of the prisoner, I'll carry out me other duties and check the premises.

PAT. Do that.

VOLUNTEER. It's only a thick would neglect his duty, sir.

PAT. Ah sure, now, you may be blamed, Einstein, but you never will be shamed.

VOLUNTEER. I hope not, sir. Of course, God gives us the brains; it's no credit to ourselves.

PAT. Well, without coming the sergeant-major on you, will you get on with what you came for?

VOLUNTEER. I will sir, directly.

He salutes smartly and marches off.

PAT. Sit down.

SOLDIER *sits by* PAT.

MISS GILCHRIST. I have such a thirst on me, I think it must be the singing. You haven't—[*she looks under the table*] oh, Mr. Pat, you gave that twelve of stout a very quick death.

PAT. You could sing that if you had an air to it. Leslie, pop down to the corner and get us a dozen of stout.

SOLDIER. Right you are, sir.

PAT. The corner shop, mind.

SOLDIER. Yes, guv.

VOLUNTEER [*entering*]. Get back there! Into the circle! Where the hell do you think you're going?

SOLDIER. He told me to—

MEG. Now, Pat, you're only going to get the boy into trouble.

PAT. Right! Attention, quick march! Stand in your circle. Right!

The VOLUNTEER *marches over to* PAT.

No, you go and sit in the circle. Leslie, you come and sit over here.

SOLDIER. You just told me to—

PAT. Never mind what I told you. Come and sit here a minute.

SOLDIER [*in circle*]. You're just leading me up the garden path, sending me out for beer, you are. An' all of a sudden I'll look round and cop a bullet in my head. Anyway, I'll tell you this much, an Englishman can die as well as an Irishman or anybody else in the world.

PAT. Don't give me all that ould stuff about dying. There's no danger of your dying this next fifty years—barring you get a belt of an atom bomb, God bless you. Come and sit down.

SOLDIER *comes.*

Finish your drink.

SOLDIER. Do you know, Paddy, up till now I've proper enjoyed myself.

PAT. 'Course you have. Good luck to you, so, cheers!

SOLDIER. You know how it is.

SOLDIER *begins to sing "When Irish Eyes are Smiling". The others join in.*

[*Aside.*] Yeah, I've had a real good time, I have, better than the square bashing.

PAT. Sure thing!

MISS GILCHRIST [*sings*].

I have no mother to break her heart
I have no father to take my part.

MEG. She's off again.

MISS GILCHRIST AND SOLDIER [*sing*].

I have one friend and a girl is she.
And she'd lay down her life for McCaffery.

MISS GILCHRIST. Jesus, Mary and Joseph, I feel for this boy as if I were his mother.

MEG. That's remarkable, that is.

MISS GILCHRIST. It would be more remarkable if I were his father.

MEG. Were his father? How many of you is there? I never heard you were married.

MISS GILCHRIST. You never heard the Blessed Virgin was married.

MEG. That was done under the Special Powers Act by the Holy Ghost.

MISS GILCHRIST. I repulse your prognostications. It would answer you better [*she points to the floor*] to go and clean your carpet.

MEG. How dare you! Men of good taste have complicated me on that carpet. Away, you scruff-hound, and thump your craw with the other hypocrites.

MISS GILCHRIST. Pray, do not insult my religiosity.

MEG. Away, you brass.

MISS GILCHRIST. I stand fast by my Lord, and will sing my hymn now.

[*Sings.*]

I love my dear Redeemer,
My creator, too, as well.
And oh, that filthy Devil,
Should stay below in Hell.
I cry to Mr. Dulles,
Please grant me this great boon,
Don't muck about, don't muck about,
Don't muck about with the moon.

I am a little Christ-ian,
My feet are white as snow.
And every day my prayers I say,
For Empire lamb I go.

PAT. No wonder, with the price of beef.

MISS GILCHRIST.

I cry unto Macmillan,
That multi-racial coon,

I love him and those above him,
But don't muck about with the moon.
Don't muck about, don't muck about,
Don't muck about with the moon.

MEG. Get off the stage, you castle Catholic bitch.

MISS GILCHRIST. She is a no-class person. Things haven't been the same since the British went.

SOLDIER. That's a very kindly song you just sang, mum. Can you tell me what those kindly bastards are going to do me in for?

MEG. Maybe you voted wrong.

SOLDIER. I'm too young to have a vote for another three years.

MEG. Well, what are you poking your nose in our affairs for?

SOLDIER. In what affairs? I never knew anything about Ireland or Cyprus, or Kenya or Jordan or any of those places.

OFFICER [*entering*]. You may learn very shortly with a bullet in the back of your head.

Enter PRINCESS GRACE, RIO RITA, MULLEADY *and the* WHORES.

PRINCESS GRACE AND WHORES. Oh, no! It's not his fault.

MULLEADY. Whose fault is it then?

MISS GILCHRIST. It's the Government's fault.

PRINCESS GRACE. Poor boy!

MULLEADY. He should never have been brought here. It means trouble. I've been feeling it all day! It's illegal.

MISS GILCHRIST. Eustace? What are you doing with those persons?

MULLEADY. Are we speaking now, Miss Gilchrist? That's a

change. Ever since you've been interested in this young man's soul, a Civil Servant's soul means nothing to you.

MISS GILCHRIST. What has happened to you?

MULLEADY. You might as well be out of the world as out of the fashion.

PRINCESS GRACE. We've made a pact.

MEG. What are they up to?

PAT. I wouldn't trust them as far as I could fling them.

MULLEADY. Yes, you can't do what you like with us.

PRINCESS GRACE. You'll find out. For those who don't understand, we'll sing our ancient song. Uncle!

RIO RITA, MULLEADY *and* PRINCESS GRACE *sing "When Socrates in Ancient Greece".*

When Socrates in Ancient Greece
Sat in his Turkish bath,
He scrubbed himself, and rubbed himself,
And steamed both fore and aft.

He sang the song the sirens sang,
With Swinburne and Shakespeare,
We're here because we're queer
Because we're queer because we're here.

The highest people of the land
Are for or they're against,
It's all the same thing at the end,
A piece of sentiment.

From Swedes so tall to Arabs small
They answer with a leer,
We're here because we're queer
Because we're queer because we're here.

PRINCESS GRACE. The trouble we had getting that past the nice Earl of Scarbrough.

MISS GILCHRIST [*at end of song*]. Leslie, come away. This is not fit company for an innocent boy.

SOLDIER. No, mum.

MISS GILCHRIST. Leave off this boy. I'm sure there's a lot of good in him and he is not used to prostitutes, male, female or Wiston Mail.

MEG. Get out, you dirty low things. A decent whore can't get a shilling with 'em.

PRINCESS GRACE. Oh, Meg Dillon, you're very bigoted.

MEG. Don't use language like that here.

PRINCESS GRACE. Ta, ta, Leslie.

MISS GILCHRIST. Leave him. This boy is not a ponce.

SOLDIER. No, I'm a builder's labourer; at least I was.

MISS GILCHRIST. Honest toil.

SOLDIER. It's a mug's game.

MISS GILCHRIST. Oh my boy! Music, please.

They sing duet to the tune of Rolling Home to Merry England, SOLDIER *speaking his lines.*

Would you live on woman's earnings?
Would you give up work for good?
For a life of prostitution,

SOLDIER. Yes, too bloody true, I would.

MISS GILCHRIST. Would you have a kip in Soho?
Would you be a West End ponce?

SOLDIER. I'm fed up with pick and shovel,
And I'd like to try it once.

MISS GILCHRIST. Did you read the Wolfenden
Report on people like these?

SOLDIER. Yes, gorblimey it was moving—
[*To* MULLEADY.] Can I borrow your copy, please?

Well, at this ponce business
I think I'll have a try.
And I'll drop the English coppers,
They are the best money can buy.

MISS GILCHRIST. Goodbye, my son, God bless you,
Say your prayers each morn and night,
And send home your poor old mother,
A few quid—her widow's mite.

Enter TERESA.

TERESA [*softly on stairs*]. Leslie!

VOLUNTEER. You can call me Feargus.

PAT [*to* VOLUNTEER]. Come out of that.

TERESA. Leslie!

PAT [*to* VOLUNTEER]. Psst. Psst. Come out of that or you'll have us in trouble.

VOLUNTEER. What?

PAT. Attention! On guard! Now take off the lights and give them a chance.

MEG, PAT, MISS GILCHRIST, VOLUNTEER, *exeunt.*

TERESA. Leslie!

SOLDIER. I'm here.

TERESA. That strict officer is coming back to relieve Pat and I won't get a chance of a word with you.

SOLDIER. Well, what do you want?

TERESA. Don't be so narky. I just wanted to see you.

SOLDIER. Well, you'd better take a good look, hadn't you?

TERESA. What's eating you? I only wanted to talk to you, that's all.

SOLDIER. You haven't got much time, have you? Because I mightn't be able to talk so well with a hole right through me head.

TERESA. Musha! Don't be talking like that.

SOLDIER. Why not? Eh, why not?

TERESA. I came to see if you wanted a cup of tea.

SOLDIER. No, thanks, I've just had a barrel of beer.

TERESA. I'll go.

SOLDIER. Just before you go, don't think you've taken me for a complete bloody fool, will you? All this tea and beer lark. You even obliged me with that [*indicates bed*] meal!

TERESA. For God's sake.

SOLDIER. Well, go and look out of that window. Can you see that man on the corner? Another one at the door opposite? There are more than these two idiots doing guard on me. Look at those two by that archway, pretending they're lovers. That should be right up your street, pretending they're lovers! That's a laugh!

TERESA. It's not my fault. I wasn't pretending.

SOLDIER. How can I believe you and your blarney?

TERESA. The boys won't harm you. Pat told me himself they only wanted to question you, and to frighten the British about the boy in Belfast.

SOLDIER. Do you think he's going to tell you the truth, or even me? After all, if you really . . . if you really felt sorry for me you might shout to the police, mightn't you?

TERESA. I'm not an informer.

SOLDIER. Don't I know it. How long have I got? What time is it?

TERESA. It's not eleven yet. I heard the quarter bell go in the city.

SOLDIER. They'll just be waking up at home, fellows will be coming out of the dance halls.

TERESA. Look at that old fellow half-jarred, sobering up for fear of what herself will say when he gets in at the door.

SOLDIER. Back home, couple of hundred miles away, might be on another bloody planet.

TERESA. Look at that, the chip shop is still open. I could pretend to go for some chips. I could . . .

SOLDIER. I don't want any chips. Could you eat if you knew you were for it? You're thinking of that poor bastard in Belfast. What about me?

TERESA. God help us all.

SOLDIER. What about me—here, now?

TERESA. If I really thought they'd do anything to you, I'd . . .

SOLDIER. If you thought. I'm a hostage, you know what that means? What's the point of taking a hostage if you don't mean to do him in?

TERESA. Leslie, if they do come for you, shout to me.

SOLDIER. Shout! I wouldn't get the chance. If they come . . .

TERESA. Well, I can't be sure. Pat said . . .

SOLDIER. Oh go away and leave me in peace. At least that bloke in Belfast has peace, and tomorrow he'll have nuns and priests and the whole works to see him on his way.

TERESA. I'll do anything for you, Leslie. What do you want?

SOLDIER. I don't want anything. I'll do the best I can on my own. Maybe I'll meet that Belfast geezer on the other side. We can have a good laugh together then.

TERESA. Here's that officer coming now. I've got to go.

SOLDIER. Teresa!

TERESA. Yes.

SOLDIER. I know I wasn't much good to you—but say "goodbye" properly, eh?

TERESA goes to his arms.

If I should get away, come and see me in Armagh.

TERESA. I will, Leslie.

SOLDIER. I'd like all the blokes in the billet to see you. 'Cos they've all got pictures on the walls—well, I never had any pictures, but now I've got you. Then we'd go to Belfast and have a bloody good time together.

TERESA. It would be lovely, astore.

SOLDIER. I'm due for a week-end's leave.

TERESA. I could pay my own way too.

SOLDIER. No, you need not.

TERESA. But I will . . . They're coming.

She goes. PAT and OFFICER are on the stairs.

OFFICER. What's she doing? Sleeping with him?

PAT. Mind your own business, she's not interfering with you. You should be in bed now, girl. Where are you going?

TERESA. I was going to the chip shop, for some chips for him.

OFFICER. You can't go out there now.

PAT quietens him.

PAT. It's too late, girl.

TERESA. It's only eleven.

PAT. It's nearer one.

TERESA. It's not the truth you're telling me.

PAT. Didn't you hear the bell strike?

TERESA. I did.

OFFICER. Enough talk. Get her to her room or I will.

TERESA. You're lying to me. The chip shop is open till twelve.

OFFICER. Go to your room.

TERESA. Do I have to, Pat?

PAT. Go to your room.

MISS GILCHRIST. What is going to happen to him, Mr. Pat?

PAT. Go to your room.

MISS GILCHRIST. Oh, Leslie, what's going to become of you?

SOLDIER. I don't know, mum. Maybe I'll be saved at the last minute or maybe I won't.

MISS GILCHRIST. I will give you my prayers.

SOLDIER. Thanks.

MISS GILCHRIST. I will give you a picture.

SOLDIER. Oh, she's nice.

MISS GILCHRIST. Oh, don't you recognize me?

SOLDIER. Oh, it's you, mum.

Enter a shadowy figure with a gun: the OFFICER.

Things might get a bit warm around here; I think you'd better go.

MISS GILCHRIST. God go with you, boy.

She goes off humming.

SOLDIER. Well, that's got rid of her—now the question is will Teresa go to the cops? Or won't she? The place is surrounded and even if Einstein is half sozzled there's the others outside. Will they shoot me? Yes! I suppose so. Would Teresa go to the cops? No!

There is a loud report off stage. The SOLDIER *flings himself on the ground. Sirens, whistles, etc., heard off-stage. Black-out.*

Blimey.

MEG. It's the police! Pat! Pat! Where are you?

PAT. I'm here. Take cover. There's a raid on.

SOLDIER. Where's Teresa?

MEG. Teresa!

PAT. I don't know. She's not here. Get down, get your head down—we're being raided, they'll open fire any minute.

MULLEADY [*up in the flies*]. Two of you stay on the roof. The rest come down through the attic with me.

PRINCESS GRACE. Six at the back and six round the front, two come through the cellar with me.

PAT. And take your partners for the eightsome reel.

MULLEADY. O'Shaunessy, shine a light for Jesus' sake.

O'SHAUNESSY [*off stage*]. I will, sir.

MULLEADY. Shine a light, I can't see a bloody thing.

O'SHAUNESSY [*off stage*]. I can't, sir, the battery's gone.

MULLEADY. To hell with the battery.

PRINCESS GRACE [*off stage*]. Come on, boys, stand by. O.K. there, we're going over.

MULLEADY [*off stage*]. Right, down you go, Shaun.

O'SHAUNESSY [*off stage*]. Will you go first, sir. I'm nervous of the height.

PRINCESS GRACE. Keep your heads down.

MULLEADY. Up de Valera—charge!

PAT. They'll have a job getting through my cellar—with the piano, the parrot and six volumes of the Encyclopaedia.

A flare is lighted. MONSEWER *comes in playing bagpipes.*
Psst. Get your head down.

MONSEWER. What?

PAT. Get your head down!—or we're dead.

MONSEWER. What's happening?

PAT. Hold on and I'll tell you. There's a raid on.

MONSEWER. Why the devil didn't you tell me? What's happening, Patrick?

He goes carefully to the window.

PAT. They're just taking the field, the secret police is ready for the kick off, but the regulars is hanging back—Mr. Mulleady has placed himself at the head of the forces of law and order—and Miss Gilchrist is bringing up his rear. Princess Grace has joined the Police, she's leading a platoon.

MONSEWER. Where's that officer chap?

PAT. He's nowhere to be seen. Disappeared, sir.

MONSEWER. Do you mean to say he's deserted in the face of fire?

PAT. They're coming in.

SOLDIER. Teresa!

MEG. Shut up or I'll plug you and your informer bitch when she comes in.

SOLDIER. Right, mum.

PAT. They're advancing. I think we've had it.

MONSEWER. Up the Republic. Don't fire till you see the whites of their eyes.

MEG. Let's run for it.

MONSEWER. Hold fast!

PAT. I'm running.

MULLEADY. Halt or I fire. Halt!

PAT. I'm halting.

PRINCESS GRACE. Charge!

Guns, machine-guns, smoke.

MONSEWER. Forward! Into the breach! Up the Republic!

SOLDIER. Up Arsenal!

MULLEADY. Hands up! We're coming in.

MONSEWER. If you come in we'll shoot the prisoner.

MEG. Yes.

TERESA [*off*]. Let him go. Leslie, run for it. Leslie, run!

SOLDIER. I'm coming, Teresa.

TERESA. Run!

Shots. SOLDIER *falls.*

MULLEADY AND PRINCESS GRACE. We're coming in.

MONSEWER. Patrick, we're surrounded.

MEG. Put that gun down or I'll kick you up the backside.

PAT, MEG, *and* MONSEWER *put their hands up.*

MONSEWER [*to* MULLEADY]. Who are you?

MULLEADY. I'm a secret policeman and I don't care who knows it. Arrest those women.

The VOLUNTEER *and* OFFICER I.R.A. *enter disguised as women.*

TERESA *runs in.*

TERESA. Where's Leslie?

PAT. He was here a minute ago.

TERESA. Where is he? Leslie!

She sees him.

MEG. There he is.

PAT. He's dead. Take his identification disc.

PRINCESS GRACE [*kneels to do so*]. I did not know he was a Catholic.

TERESA. I gave it him. Leave it with him.

MULLEADY. Cover him up.

TERESA. Leslie—my love—a thousand blessings go with you.

PAT. Don't cry, Teresa—and don't blame anybody for it. Nobody meant to kill him.

TERESA. But he's dead.

PAT. And so is the boy in Belfast Jail.

TERESA. Ah, it was not Belfast Jail or the six counties that was bothering you—but your lost youth and your crippled leg. I will never forget him. He died in a strange land and at home he has no one. I will never forget you, Leslie. Never, till the end of time. [*She turns away.*]

SOLDIER [*sings*].

The bells of hell
Go ting-a-ling-a-ling
For you but not for me.
Oh death where is thy
Sting-a-ling-a-ling
Or grave thy victory?
If you meet the undertaker
Or the young man from the Pru,
Get a pint with what's left over.
Now I'll say goodbye to you.